DUTY IS OURS, RESULTS ARE GOD'S

God Bless you, Tom!

Ron Jansen

Proverbs 3:5-6

DUTY IS OURS, RESULTS ARE GOD'S

A Marine's Story Of Duty
and His Search For Truth

CAPTAIN RANDALL JANSEN, USMC Retired

TATE PUBLISHING
AND **ENTERPRISES**, LLC

Published by Tate Publishing & Enterprises, LLC
127 E. Trade Center Terrace | Mustang, Oklahoma 73064 USA
1.888.361.9473 | www.tatepublishing.com

Tate Publishing is committed to excellence in the publishing industry. The company reflects the philosophy established by the founders, based on Psalm 68:11,
"The Lord gave the word and great was the company of those who published it."

Published in the United States of America

ISBN: 978-1-63185-331-9
1. Biography & Autobiography / Personal Memoirs
2. Religion / Christian Life / Personal Growth
14.07.08

DEDICATION

John Q. Adams, the 6th US President and son of John Adams, the 2nd US President, when contemplating the long, arduous, struggle for life, liberty and freedom said this: "Duty is ours, results are Gods."

When I look back over my seventy plus years, I realize that this concept provides a great way to live. If we will commit ourselves to doing the duty for which God has prepared and equipped each of us, we will have inner peace, joy and contentment. Regardless of the pressures, troubles and seemingly overwhelming obstacles we face in this world, we can be assured our Sovereign God is in absolute control of all results.

I have a deep sense of respect and thankfulness to all those in the past, and those today, who have committed their lives and fortunes to the principles of freedom and liberty that we all enjoy. I dedicate this book to all of those and to God who made it all possible.

ACKNOWLEDGMENTS

Most authors mention a person or two who have been helpful or instrumental in the writing of their book. I would like to acknowledge everyone I have ever met, beginning, of course, with my parents, grandparents, my brother and sister, all my aunts and uncles, cousins, in-laws (including three sailors), neighbors, classmates, teachers, professors, instructors, preachers, bosses, friends, and acquaintances—all of whom have been valuable in my life and development. All have left impressions from which I have learned a great deal.

I want to give special thanks to all the doctors, nurses, corpsmen, and therapists who performed their tasks with perfection during my surgeries, treatment, and therapy.

Obviously, the Marine Corps and all the marines (from privates to generals) that I knew had a huge influence upon my life; I thank them all for their service to our country and in being a part of my life—I'll never forget them or the corps we served.

My wife, Diane, and my two children, Theresa and Craig, have been more than wonderful. These three are at the top of my list of those I want around in any life situation, fun times or in tough spots. They have made my life rich.

Thanks also go to the authors of all the works mentioned in my bibliography. Their scholarly works are informative, enlightening and inspiring.

Finally, because he put it all together, I want to thank God. God is the source of life, truth, love, grace, mercy, joy, peace, protection, guidance, correction, comfort, justice, fulfillment, blessings, and every good thing. I also want to thank God for allowing the tough spots and difficulties into my life; without those, I would never have learned to seek him or trust him.

The New International Version of the Bible is used in all quotations of scripture.

ONE

The navy doctor had just walked out of my room aboard the USS *Repose*, a navy hospital ship off the coast of Vietnam. His words left me stunned, "After surgery tomorrow, you will have limited use of your left shoulder and arm, and your marine career is finished."With that, he turned and left; there was no explanation or discussion. The problem with my left shoulder and arm is not what I focused on—the part about my life as a marine being over was the devastating news. Some birthday present! The day was May 2, 1966, my twenty-fourth birthday.

The news the doctor gave me was totally unexpected. I had no idea of the direction my life would take, but I had a deep feeling of peace and joy in that I was convinced God was not surprised by any of this; he still had a plan for my life. One thing I was sure of was that I was going to have a lot of time over the next few weeks to contemplate how I arrived where I was and what would be coming next.

This life-changing event began late afternoon on April 29. I'd just taken a shower and was lying on my cot in a tent I shared with other marine helicopter pilots at Chu Lai, South Vietnam. I decided to wait for someone to come along to go to the mess tent with me. A moment later our squadron duty officer came by and asked if I'd mind flying copilot on a re-supply mission. It was my policy to never miss a chance for action, so I grabbed my weapon and helmet and ran down to the flight line to fly my 248th mission. The helicopter was already running with rotor engaged as I scrambled up the side into the left seat. I strapped in and plugged my helmet into the intercom system. "You have it," the pilot said. "I have it," I responded.

I grabbed the controls, applied take-off power, and lifted off. I glanced at the instruments as we passed 1,250 feet, doing ninety knots—all was fine. Suddenly there was a loud crashing noise—I told myself that we were taking fire, that I was hit and that I "really got it this time." (I had been wounded with minor shrapnel wounds on two prior occasions.) My left hand and forearm, which had been on the throttle and collective pitch stick, was now lying on my lap; my fingers were moving outside of my control. My next thought was that my arm had been shot off and that it would fall between my body and the collective stick and thereby prevent the other pilot from controlling the helicopter. As I picked up my left arm at the wrist, I realized that my arm was still attached at the shoulder. Blood was everywhere; I could also feel it running down my left side. My next thought was that I probably would be dead or at least unconscious in a minute or two. I couldn't remember if I had locked my harness; the take-off had been immediate after I had climbed into the cockpit, and I hadn't gone through the checklist.

The locking lever was on the left side of my seat, but I couldn't reach it with my right hand. As I struggled to reach across my useless left arm, I was concerned that when I died, I would fall over the cyclic stick and the other pilot would completely lose control of the helicopter. As my struggle to reach the lever continued, I wondered how my family and unofficial fiancée were going to take the news of my death. I had no fear; I knew where I was going, I believed I would be in heaven before the helicopter got back to the base. This belief was not based on my having been "good enough" or that I had given enough or prayed enough or had done enough "religious activities" to have earned it. I knew I was going to heaven because Jesus Christ, the Son of God, had paid for my sin in full.

Suddenly I became furious, livid, hopping mad. At that point I knew I wasn't going to die—at that time anyway. In a couple of minutes, the pilot landed at the medical landing zone. The crew chief/gunner came up the side of the helicopter and in a feat of strength and balance, lifted me out of the cockpit and carried me back down the side of the helicopter. For a moment the first feeling of fear hit me: I was afraid he was going to drop me on my head and do more damage.

Seconds later I was in a meat truck (ambulance), bouncing up the gravel road to the medical tent; pain was now making its presence felt. A moment later my flight suit was being cut off. At some point in the process, I received a shot of morphine. By the time the squadron commanding officer and my longtime friend from flight school arrived, I had a big smile on my face and was feeling no pain. The last thing I remember anyone saying was that the doctor would work on me as soon as he finished another case. When I woke up, I noticed I was in a Quonset hut with cots along both walls, all occupied by wounded marines. I saw a navy corpsman sitting at a desk to my right. "Hey, Doc, when are they going to operate on me?" I asked. I was informed I had been operated on six hours earlier.

April 30 was a blur. On May 1st, a major general came by to present Purple Hearts to the marines in the ward. Later, two marines from my squadron came by and presented me with the bullet that passed through my shoulder and got stuck in the seat. They informed me that I probably had been hit by an AK-47. The first of a five round burst went into my arm and through my shoulder, the other four bullets went into the panel behind my head. After that, my doctor came by to tell me my shoulder was too unstable for me to travel home and that I would be sent out to the USS *Repose* for further surgery. Going home? I wasn't ready to go home. I had no idea of the extent of my injury, nor did I even think to ask.

The next day I was flown out to the *Repose*. I hadn't been on the ship an hour when a Red Cross volunteer showed up with cake, ice cream, and a birthday card. I was impressed. An hour later the doctor who was to do the surgery the next day had also come and gone.

Life aboard the *Repose* following surgery was uneventful. Reading, visiting, and helping each other cut up food at dinner was all there was. Another lieutenant had his right arm shot up, so between the two of us, we had one good pair of arms—his left and my right.

Two weeks later I began the trip to the hospital at the Great Lakes Navel Training Center, Illinois. A helicopter ride from the *Repose* to Da Nang was followed by a twin-engine turbo-prop ride to Clark AFB in the Philippines, where we stayed overnight. The next day we left Clark on a C-141 Starlifter, which would take us to Hawaii and then on to Travis AFB in California. Sometime after leaving Clark, one of the engines went out, so we spent the night in Guam.

From Guam, we went on to Hawaii where we landed for fuel at about 1:00 a.m. There were army, navy, air force, and marine wounded on the aircraft. Only one of the four services had a representative to meet the plane and greet its people: the US Marine Corps. I was amazed and gratified to see a marine major general come through the plane, shaking the hand of each marine, asking how we were doing, thanking us for our service, and wishing us well. This was just another one of those little things that I experienced in the Marine Corps that sets the corps apart from every other organization I've been familiar with in my lifetime.

The navy doctors and corpsmen also impressed me with their care and concern. Another group of people who need honorable mention are the air crews, nurses, hospital personnel, and everyone having a part in the medical evacuation and transportation of our wounded warriors; they all did an outstanding job. Whether we were in a bus, plane, hospital, or anywhere in between, we never missed a shot, pill, or treatment. These were the highly skilled and very compassionate people of the US Air Force.

We spent a night at Travis AFB in California, and the next day began the final leg of our trip home. We arrived at the NAS (Naval Air Station) Glenview in Illinois at night to sounds of protesters screaming at us. One of the marines taking us from the air station to the Great Lakes Naval Hospital wanted to go out to the fence and "take out" a few of the protesters. I would have liked to go with him, but cooler heads prevailed. Besides, I was on a stretcher.

What a trip that had been! I arrived at my temporary home on the ninth floor of the navy hospital where nurses and corpsman hustled about to make us as comfortable as possible. The war was a long way off, and whatever was coming next I didn't know. I felt as though I had reached a milestone of some sort. I was content.

TWO

The two weeks aboard the USS *Repose* had provided a lot of time to ponder my beginnings and the path I had taken. My first thoughts went back to my parents in Holland, Michigan. Ben and Alice Jansen were the best parents one could hope for—hardworking and dedicated to God, family, and country. My dad was a machinist, and mom, a full-time wife, mother, and homemaker. I had two younger siblings: a brother, Ben, and a sister, Alene. I'm proud of all of them.

In addition to family, music, fishing, and baseball, the Bible, and church were the focal points of our lives. On Sunday, there were morning and evening services plus Sunday school. During the school year, the three of us attended the Holland Christian Schools from K-12. By the time I graduated from high school in 1960, I probably had a great deal more Bible and theology training than one would have had after a few years of Bible school. We knew a lot of stuff. Unfortunately, learning a lot of stuff can be a problem. I believe knowledge is very good, necessary in fact to prevent bad doctrine and cult involvement. On the other hand, knowledge of facts can lead to a lot of religious pride and religious rules, the opposite of what God wants, which is godly character. Fortunately, my folks provided a great example of practical Christianity; they obviously trusted God and had a relationship with him. It was through their example that I found a relationship with God, even though it was tarnished by "religiosity."

As I grew up, a great deal of thought was put into the concept of finding the will of God for ones life (ie, There is only one career that God wants for a person, and one had better find it). I believe more emphasis should have been placed on the concept of having a relationship with Jesus and developing a godly character. This would solve a lot of problems and provide one with more peace and joy. Somehow as a youngster, I developed the idea that if one really wanted to serve God, there were only two possible jobs: either a pastor or missionary; anything other than these two jobs made a person a second-class Christian. After having seen and heard missionaries in church and in school, the problem was solved for me. Generally the missionaries I met seemed to be an unhappy, joyless group that never mentioned hunting, fishing, and sports. That did it for me. There was only one choice, and that was to be a pastor. With that in mind, in the fall of 1960, I became a pre-seminary student at Calvin College in Grand Rapids, Michigan. Four years of college and three years of seminary lie ahead. However, thirty seconds after the registration process was complete, I knew I was in trouble. On the way home (I commuted with four other Calvin students, one a second-year pre-seminary student), I knew the trouble was even deeper than I thought. I found that in four years of pre-seminary, there was only one class in the sophomore year that I cared for—the rest were a bust. I put on a pretty good show, did the work, and achieved good grades; but I knew this was not for me. Also, at that time, the Russians and the United States were growling at each other. I didn't want there to be a war, but if there was going to be one, I didn't want to miss it either. One afternoon in the spring, I walked to the marine recruiter in Grand Rapids. My favorite uncle had extolled the glories of the corps to me since I was little, so there was no consideration of any other of the armed forces. One of the best things that I picked up at college was that God wanted his people in many different careers and that one was not any better or "more religious" than the others. Regardless of one's profession or station in life, all positions are spiritually equal before the Lord. A short time later, a notice appeared on the bulletin board stating that any student not returning to Calvin the next fall for any reason should make an appointment with the dean; this I did.

A few days later I walked in to the dean's office. "What are you going to do? Are you going to Hope College (a sister college in my hometown) next fall?" he asked. "No, I'm joining the Marine Corps," I replied. The dean was shocked into silence. I guess this was the first time a pre-seminary student with good grades had left school for the Marine Corps. He sent me to the school psychologist to take some aptitude tests. I scored high in military, sports, and outdoor activities such as game warden. The doctor also thought it was a good idea to go to the corps. I definitely wasn't ready for college.

In Detroit, Michigan, on July 3, 1961, I was sworn in as a private in the marines. The backslapping, handshaking, smiley-faced marines who helped us with the paperwork and swearing in had become instant friends. I assumed that more of the same would greet us at the Marine Corps recruit depot in San Diego, California. I further assumed that since we would be arriving in San Diego on our nation's independence day that there would be a picnic with plenty of basketball and baseball games. The recruiter had told me that the marines are big into sports, which is true. I also assumed that there would be a tour of the base and the training facilities with friendly marines. I was wrong.

The evening of July 3, the marines placed me in charge of a dozen or so recruits and dropped us off at the Detroit airport for our flight to San Diego. I was excited, to say the least; I had never been on a plane before and seldom far from my home. At age sixteen, I made a bear-hunting trip to Michigan's Upper Peninsula, and at seventeen, I made a canoe trip into Canada. Other than that, I had little experience outside of Holland, Michigan. The next morning, I was delighted and excited as we flew over the desert southwest; the cacti, rocks, and mountains intrigued me. Anticipation of marine training and becoming a marine filled me with a spirit of excitement and adventure. I knew the next four months would be tough; however, I love new experiences and adventures. I always wanted to see what was beyond the next bend in the river or over the next hill.

As the leader of the Detroit recruits, I had been given a number to call upon our arrival in San Diego. After hanging up the phone, I had an uneasy feeling about what awaited us. The marine on the phone did not sound at all like any of the backslapping, handshaking, smiley-faced marines I had known in Grand Rapids and Detroit. He told me to wait in front of the terminal. I had the recruits in two lines at the front of the terminal when a few minutes later, a grey marine bus pulled up, and a marine gunnery sergeant (a gunny) leaped out and began shouting. He told us to get onto the bus and that there would be no talking, gum-chewing, or smoking. He used many other words, most of which I had heard working in a large commercial bakery in Holland while attending high school. I was astonished at the gunny's vocabulary. In that one sentence he told us to get into the bus, he used every naughty word that I ever heard, some of which were placed in between syllables of legitimate words. I was about to ask him if his mother knew he talked like that but I thought better of it and shut up. At this point, I had no idea of what awaited us at the end of this bus trip, but I was sure of a few things; I was sure there would be no basketball, baseball, or watermelon. I also knew I was no longer in charge of the other recruits; in fact, I was no longer in charge of myself. As we were waved through the gate by a corporal with a big smile—actually, more of a smirk—I knew my life was going to be changed forever. As the bus came to a stop, the gunny began shouting for us to move out of the bus and get into the line of recruits standing at attention with their suitcases by their sides. I dashed out of the bus, stopping behind the last man and placed my suitcase by my side, then I snapped to attention. Immediately, a terrorist in a Marine uniform was screaming into my ear, questioning why I had set my suitcase on the deck (ground) without permission. For a minute or two, we played the "pick it up and put it down game." He then informed me that if I ever did anything again without permission, he would jump onto my shoulders and unscrew my head. He added a comment or two about what he would do after that, but we'll leave it there. I heard two other drill instructors (DIs) talking loudly enough for us to hear. They were complaining about the low quality of recruits that were coming in and were wondering about how anybody could expect anybody to turn this bunch of society dredges and mothers mistakes into marines. At this point, I believed that there had been a mistake. I assumed that they were mistakenly anticipating a bunch of kids from jail and reform schools because twenty-four hours earlier, we were told that we were the cream of American youth and that the Marine Corps was glad to have us. I assumed that this problem would be taken care of, but I also knew no one there was interested in me pointing this out to them.

At this time, I would like to share a few thoughts about the lessons that can be learned. First, be careful about assuming things, especially if you are about to move into a new circumstance or situation, be it a new job, school, marriage, or anything different from your past. By keeping calm, mouth shut, ears and eyes open, one can learn a lot that will help not only in overcoming tough situations but in developing character that will help us become effective in what it is we have to do. The Marine Corps knows how to take a bunch of kids and turn them into the finest fighting fraternity that has ever existed. God knows how to take a totally flawed human being and turn that human into a bearer of his own image to be effective in his kingdom; this is not without pain and suffering. Often we will not know what he is up to, but if we accept our circumstances and situation, learn from it, and continue to look to him, we will do more than survive—we will be successful, not as the world sees success, but as he sees it for us.

Secondly, be open to new ideas and concepts, don't be locked into a way of thinking or doing—be open, learn, observe, think, and evaluate. No matter how smart, educated, or experienced one is, there are things to learn, ways to become better and more valuable. I had no idea of what I had gotten myself into, but I trusted the United States of America and the United States Marine Corps to do the right thing. I also had been taught to trust God in all things, now I was about to find out about that. I assure you that God is much more trustworthy and perfect in all his ways than anything in this world. I would learn a lot in the next four months. It was an experience I wouldn't want to do again if it only cost a nickel, but I wouldn't give up the experience for a million dollars. Stories of boot camp are numerous, and many are hilariously funny, perhaps not at the time, but looking back it sometimes cracks me up.

There is one thing I have never forgotten, and much can be said about it, but I'll cover it later in the book. We had returned from the rifle range a week or two before, and the overall attitude of the DIs was a little different. We had a week or two to go to graduation. Although the physical rough stuff had not changed, the DIs began to exhibit what resembled human characteristics. In fact, by this time, most of us believed that perhaps we were not going to be killed and eaten after all. The senior DI almost seemed a little bit fatherly to us in giving council and advice about our lives in the Marine Corps post-boot camp. He mentioned that he had a wife and son living with him in nearby San Diego. This came as a bit of a surprise to me, up until that time I assumed the Marine Corps kept him in a cage somewhere on the base and just turned him loose when it was time for us to be pounded into the dirt. Speaking of being pounded into the dirt reminds me of a couple of hours in about our fourth week of training. One night after lights out, several recruits were goofing off in our squad bay, a Quonset hut that housed twenty recruits. Suddenly the door opened and there was the senior DI, "You —— people want to play —— games? We'll play —— games tomorrow after —— noon!" And play games we did. After about an hour of the "games," I was afraid I was going to die. After two hours of the "games" I was afraid I wasn't going to die. At the close of the games, as I was doing push-ups, the drill instructor had his foot between my shoulder blades; the harder I tried to push-up, the harder he pushed down. He eventually pushed my face into the dirt. Even though he won, I didn't feel beaten. To me this became the highlight of boot camp training. Yes, we learned first aid, how to take care of and shoot our weapons, Marine Corps history, and many other things; but the most important lesson in all of boot camp and life is this: never quit, give it everything you have, and then some more. The attitude that has made the Marine Corps one of the most successful, most feared military organizations in history is simply this: "you may kill us, but you'll never beat us."

As Christians, we need this attitude also. We face a shooting war against radical Islam, a cultural war, and a constant battle between the flesh and the spirit within ourselves. Our attitude should be "victory at any cost."

One evening, as we all sat around at ease, the senior DI was going on about being a marine and what to expect in the corps. He said there were three priorities in the life of a marine: God, country, and corps. At the time, I was probably too young and ignorant to fully appreciate the implications of what he said; looking back I see this as a monumental proposition. If there is no God, then the concept of having anything other than oneself as being a priority is pure madness; the concepts of service, commitment, and self-sacrifice, are nonsense if there is no God.

Following graduation, we went to Camp Pendleton for a month of infantry training. All marines, whatever their military specialty, are expected to be basic infantry marines. The atmosphere was a little more relaxed than boot camp, and for the first time, we were called marines instead of —— worms, screws, bugs, etc.

We spent time in the field, fired automatic weapons and flamethrowers, threw hand grenades, crawled through infiltration courses with live automatic rifle fire overhead while explosives blew up in pits around us. We also learned infantry tactics of the fire team and squad. This was tough, but it sure beat studying Latin and Greek in college.

After a twenty day leave in Holland, I reported back to Camp Pendleton and spent several months as a basic marine. I enjoyed Southern California, the ocean, the recreational facilities on base and, of course, Disneyland.

THREE

By April 1962, I had been selected for flight training and was sent to the Pensacola NAS in Florida. I was now a MARCAD (marine aviation cadet) and began sixteen weeks of pre-flight and officer training. Academics included math, physics, aerodynamics, meteorology, physiology, engineering, naval law, and Navy and Marine Corps history.

The physical training included running, calisthenics, gymnastics, trampoline, wrestling, and a lot of swimming. Along with the swimming was water survival, which included a trip to the bottom of the swimming pool. One was strapped into a cockpit, which then slid down a ramp into the pool. As the cockpit hit the pool, it flipped upside down and sank. There was a proper sequence of steps one had to take to exit the cockpit; getting the sequence wrong could cost one's life in a real situation. Another exercise involved being placed in a parachute harness, which was attached by a cable to an engine. One was then dragged through the water at high speed simulating having ejected into the ocean under windy conditions. Getting the disconnect procedure wrong could result in death. I thought this was great sport and was very happy that I wasn't being bored to death in college.

Daily inspections were another experience of preflight. Each morning we were inspected by marine drill instructors or upper-class men who quizzed us on the chain of command personalities, current events, or crazy things like "What would you do if your were on the parade field and saw a battleship sail by?" The correct answer was "I'd have another drink and watch the whole fleet go by." Uniforms, shoes, and brass buckles were all minutely examined; for example, a fingerprint on the back side of one's buckle could cost five demerits and a loss of Saturday afternoon liberty.

Daily room inspections were yet another way to apply pressure to see how we would react to a constant stream of activities. Each room had three or four cadets, and each was assigned a shelf in the room's medicine chest. All shaving cream cans had to be pointing in the same direction, as did all the toothbrushes and toothpaste tubes. All objects had to be in a descending order from the tallest to the shortest. Here again, one mistake could cost all of the occupants five demerits and the loss of a Saturday afternoon liberty. A soap bubble on a shaving cream can, a hair on a comb, or a speck of toothpaste on a toothbrush were all equally horrifying to the inspectors.

In the closets, all clothes on hangers had to be equidistant. In the chest of drawers, all socks, underwear, and shirts had to be precisely folded and lying in the correct order with equal spacing. Three mistakes in a week was costly for all the room occupants.

All of this, of course, was designed to create teamwork, interdependence, and attention to detail, which becomes very important when one finds himself in a cockpit loaded with dials, switches, gauges, and instruments. It was obvious that those responsible for teaching young people how to fly very dangerous and expensive aircraft knew what it took to get the job done. Often we fail to realize that our Creator also knows what we need to get us where he wants us to be. All we go through on this fallen earth is designed to develop character in order for us to be useful in his army.

In September, I began flying the T-34 aircraft and fortunately, I had an outstanding marine captain as a flight instructor. We had half a day of ground school and half a day of flying. In October, as I was completing primary flight training, I met the girl who would become my wife. I was invited one Saturday evening to a Youth for Christ meeting in Pensacola. As I walked down the steps into the basement for punch and cookies, I spotted her in the crowd; I knew instantly I wanted to meet her. Diane Maloy and I were married a mere forty-five months later.

The whole flight school experience offered many challenges, hard work, and a great deal of excitement. The single most exhilarating event was carrier qualifying aboard the USS *Lexington*. At this time, we were flying the T-28 fighter/bomber with a 1500-horsepower engine. Four of us, each alone in our plane, flew from a base near Pensacola out into the Gulf of Mexico to rendezvous with the carrier, which looked awfully small from several thousand feet up. After making several touch-and-go landings, each of us dropped the tail hook and made six arrested landings.

As we flew back to the base, I was much higher than my plane. I have never felt such a degree of euphoria in all my life. *Wow, if my family and friends could see me now,* I thought. At that moment, someone spoke to me. I was alone in the plane and what I heard did not come through my headset or my ears, but there was no mistaking the words: "Where would you be if you did not have perfect vision?" the voice asked. Instantly I was back in the cockpit, and the euphoria evaporated. The next question came in the same calm, non-condemning, non-confrontational voice: "Where would you be if you did not have excellent hand-eye coordination?" Where indeed! Did I do anything to get or earn my vision and coordination? Obviously, *no*!

I had been taught, since I was a little guy, that God's grace was unmerited favor. I had known the catechism answer to that question for years. Now I really knew the answer! Whatever abilities, talents, or skills we have come from God and are not meant for our own private use but are to be given back to him to use in whatever plan he has for us. None of us have anything to say about how we are blessed, whatever we have we didn't earn it or deserve it. Everything we are and have belongs to him, thus anything less than 100 percent commitment to him is totally outrageous. From that point on, I have made an effort (not always successful) to be very grateful and appreciative of everything in life. It is impossible to be thankful and content in life if there is complaining going on.

Following carrier qualification, I went on to multi-engine and instrument training and then to helicopter training, completing the flight program in January 1964. My parents came down from Michigan to pin gold second lieutenant bars on my shoulders and gold naval aviator wings on my chest. What lie ahead, I didn't know; but the feeling of adventure and excitement filled me.

In February 1964, I reported to the MCAF (Marine Corps Air Facility) New River, North Carolina. I drove into nearby Jacksonville, on Saturday night, reported into the MCAF duty officer, and then drove around the town and surrounding area. I was not impressed. At 0800 Monday morning, I reported to the personnel officer of Marine Air Group 26, a friendly major who asked me if I had any preference in my assignment to any particular helicopter squadron aboard the base. "Yes, sir," I replied. "I'd like to be in the squadron that is getting ready to deploy." He laughed and told me to come back in half an hour. He would see what he could do.

A half hour later, I found out I was the newest member of Sub Unit 2 of HMM-262, which would be deploying to the Mediterranean Sea for six months beginning in May. For the first thirty-one months I had been a trainee, now I was entering the FMF (Fleet Marine Force) as a member of the world's finest, most feared, fighting force. Yes, I was an inexperienced, brand new, most junior rank, needs-a-lot-of-training, doesn't-know-what's-going-on, youngest pilot in the squadron.

Up until now, it was all school, now the real adventure and excitement was about to begin.

The rest of the day was spent checking into the squadron, getting a room at the BOQ (Bachelor Officer Quarters), and familiarization of the base. The next morning, I made my first appearance to the entire squadron and was introduced at the APM (All Pilot's Meeting). I had been told in flight school that naval aviators were above average in intelligence; I don't know about that, but what I am sure about is that most naval aviators are way above average in crazy. The meeting was being conducted by the operations officer, a major, who introduced the new member 2/LT Randall "Ran" Jansen. Immediately, a lieutenant jumped to his feet and shouted "*Let's sing him a hymn!*" I thought, *What is this all about?* At that point, the entire squadron sang loudly and out of tune, "Hymnnn-Hymnnn——Himmm."

Like July 1961, I wondered what on earth I had gotten into, that was definitely a first as was everything else that was to happen in the next six years. After the meeting, each member of the squadron welcomed me with handshakes, backslaps, and big grins; I felt accepted as a full-fledged member of the squadron, there was never any hazing. Among the members I met that morning was the Beaver, the Bear, the Fox, Packy (the Pachyderm), Tex, the Mouth (the one who directed the singing of the hymn), Wildcat, and Quiz (*why* was his favorite word). I came to find out that if there were any shenanigans, laughing, or crazy stuff going on, Beaver, Packy, Tex, or the Mouth were probably somewhere near by. I resolved to stay out of the craziness, and I did very well in avoiding the horseplay, shenanigans, and craziness most of the time—well, maybe one time I avoided it.

To be a contributing member of the squadron required a lot of training before deployment, but I was treated as a full member of the squadron, and everyone pitched in and got me ready in a short time. These marine pilots were a mixed bunch from many different backgrounds, there were no two alike, but in many ways, they were the same. Generally, they were adventurous, professional, committed, fun-loving, and a little wild and crazy. I cannot think of one that I would not trust my life with in a flight, fight, war, or survival situation.

In May, the twenty pilots of the sub-unit flew by C-130 to Spain where we boarded the USS *Donner*, which would be our home for the next six adventurous months.

FOUR

The six months on the Mediterranean cruise was a great adventure, from Barcelona, Spain to Tekagac, Turkey with many places in between; this cruise was the trip of a lifetime. In Rome, Italy, I visited the usual sights, including the Coliseum, the Vatican, and the catacombs where the early Christians lived, met, hid out, and were buried. The Vatican, with its spectacular design, artifacts and art was another world. Being a Christian, I found it easier to identify with the Christianity of the catacombs than that of the Vatican. Jesus said that his kingdom was not of this world and those who followed him would suffer persecution. The opulent trappings of the Vatican appeared to me to be an aberration of what Jesus is all about. The Vatican was awesome, the catacombs deeply moving.

When the fleet put into Venice, Italy, I took some leave and went by train to Geneva, Switzerland. After a few days of visiting the sights in Geneva, I flew to the Netherlands, my mother's homeland, there I met some of her family and visited her hometown. Several of my mother's family were killed fighting tyranny in World War II. From that, I was taught the importance of standing up for real peace and freedom.

From the Netherlands, I flew to Paris, and after a few days there, I flew to meet the fleet in Barcelona, Spain. We also visited Palma, Malta, France, Greece, and Sicily. Usually there were day tours to visit the countryside to explore local cultures, which was a great learning experience. In Palma de Mallorca, I went to see the bull fights. Before the first fight was over, I was out of there; I was thoroughly disgusted. Several years later, I ran into another marine who had gone to the bull fights in the same place with a group of marines. He told me the marines caused a great disturbance by cheering for the bull.

There was also work to be done. The reason for our being there was to "fly the flag," train, and be ready for any conflict in the area. Military operations are inherently dangerous, and there is a price to pay. During our cruise, we lost three Marines, two in ground training operations and one who went down with a helicopter that crashed into the sea. The price of freedom is high, a fact that we often forget in our busy, materialistic lifestyle. Whether it is political freedom or spiritual freedom, there is no peace or freedom without the shedding of blood.

The flying was varied and a great experience for a young newcomer like me. Transporting marines from ship to shore on practice assaults, landing on unprepared sites, practice instrument flying, formation flying, and even a medical evacuation for an injured marine to Athens, Greece, were a part of our flying duties. With gas to burn and plenty of time, we also looked for other opportunities. One of our favorite activities was to put on air shows for villagers and beachgoers. These shows were, of course, unofficial, unapproved, and, well, illegal. One day we were flying in a four helo formation when the flight leader saw a beach front resort up ahead. He signaled us into a tight diamond formation, and we made a low pass in front of the beachgoers. Let me point out that the flight rules said something about being a half mile from an occupied beach and at least five hundred feet above the water. Anyway, as we roared past the beach, I could clearly see what the lifeguard on the tower was wearing (he was at eye level with us), and I had to look up a little to see the people sipping their drinks on the veranda of the hotel.

Unfortunately for us, one of the hotel guests was a navy captain, a naval aviator who knew the rules. He sent a message to our CO explaining what he had seen. He made some remark about the fact that although he could only estimate our distance from the beach and our altitude, the noise of our engines interrupted his conversation inside the hotel and that our rotor wash was clearly visible on the water. He also warned of the consequences of future incidents. Our CO was very unhappy and put us out of the air show business for the rest of the cruise. In short, I was having the time of my life. I would have made this cruise for free! Seeing all the sights, flying, and associating with a great group of marines was better than anything I could have imagined.

One event that summer had a huge and permanent impact on my life. Vietnam was mentioned more and more, and one day I saw a magazine, on the cover was a picture of a dead marine helicopter pilot lying on the floor of his helicopter. He had been shot in Vietnam. That did it for me. That day I had a letter on the way to the CO of MAG-26 (Marine Air Group) requesting assignment to the next squadron leaving for Vietnam. I had no idea who the pilot was; all I knew was that the communists who have no regard for life or freedom had killed a brother of mine.

Upon our return to New River in November, the CO of HMM-262 called me to his office and informed me the next squadron going to Vietnam was HMM-263 and that they were deploying in the summer of 1965. He also said that he was taking HMM-262 to the Caribbean for a three-month cruise beginning in January 1965, and that he needed me. He asked me if I would be willing to go with him. I was stunned! He certainly didn't have to ask, he didn't even have to talk to me. This was the epitome of leadership in my mind. He let me know I was valuable and that he really cared about me as an individual—a trait I saw in all the COs I had in the corps. "Yes, sir. I will go with you", I responded.

In January 1965, the CO pinned silver first lieutenant bars on my shoulders. A week later we embarked on the USS *Guadalcanal*, a helicopter carrier built from the keel up to transport an infantry battalion and helicopter squadron to fight anywhere in the world. We were headed to the Caribbean for a three month cruise to "fly the flag," train, and be ready for any contingency in that area—an area known for trouble throughout the years. The battalion and squadron that replaced us in late April suffered casualties in fighting that broke out in the Dominican Republic.

Generally, in my marine career, I got along well with the navy. The six months in the Mediterranean as well as my year and a half in flight school were great. The three-month Caribbean cruise was a different matter entirely; it started bad and finished worse. I thought the whole thing was hilarious.

There is a great deal of danger involved with military operations, and we were headed into an area known for trouble. We marines thought at some point the captain of the ship would give us a friendly "welcome aboard" and perhaps a comment or two about working together in a dangerous environment. Wrong! Within an hour of the last marine boarding the ship, the captain was on the PA, obviously irritated with a strong edge in his voice. "This is the captain speaking. While you marines are aboard my ship, you will use naval terminology such as bulkhead (wall), overhead (ceiling), deck (floor), and ladder (stairway)." We had three dangerous months ahead, and this guy was concerned about using naval terminology which we all knew. One thing I had seen in marines during my short career is that they are well disciplined, quick to obey orders, and very military; they are also a bunch of rebels, especially to someone outside of their ranks whom they don't like. In short, this captain had declared war. I have never seen eighteen hundred marines get agitated that quickly.

That evening all the marine officers were informed that if we wanted to eat, we needed to join the mess. I have been on five ships in my career, but this was the only time I had to "join the mess." Seventy dollars was a good piece of change in those days. We were told we would have equal share in the mess with the navy officers. A few days later, we were to find out exactly how "equal" we were.

The next evening, the wardroom (officers' lounge) next to the dining hall was full of marine and navy officers. On the bulkhead, in the wardroom, was a glass case containing a long, narrow flag. In a booming voice, Tex asked, "What's that ol' rag y'all have in the case on the wall?" The words *rag* and *wall*, I believe, were emphasized, but I could be wrong. He was informed, rather stiffly I observed, that this was the ships commissioning pennant on the bulkhead.

Minutes later another marine (a tall fellow from one of the Great Lakes states, I recall) added fuel to the fire by asking about a large volleyball trophy being displayed in the wardroom. The question was "What did you guys do, beat a bunch of Virginia Beach Girl Scouts in volleyball?" The stiff, icy response was that they were the volleyball champions of the amphibious fleet, Atlantic. The marine response was that a pick-up team from the squadron could beat them anytime.

That evening, the marines were informed that beginning the next day, marines would eat at the first seating while the navy would eat an hour later. Following dinner the next evening, we marines retired to our ready room where we were briefed for missions, had meetings, watched movies, and hung out. We were all growling and complaining about the horrible meal we had just eaten. Unknown to us, our squadron duty officer had been about the ship on some mission while we ate, and he had gone to eat with the navy at the second sitting. Shortly thereafter, he sauntered into the ready room whistling a happy tune.

"What are you so happy about, Jim?" growled the colonel.

"Just had a great meal, Colonel!" Jim replied enthusiastically.

"That's not even funny!" snorted the colonel.

"What do you mean, sir?" the puzzled lieutenant asked.

"What do you mean? What did you have?" the colonel fired back.

"Steak, potatoes, and veg—"

The colonel shot out of that room. I don't know who he tangled with, but that was the end of grub for marines and food for sailors.

A day or two later, the captain was again on speaker. "Don't you marines know how to take a navy shower? You are using too much fresh water!" A couple of days later we found out that some plumbing had been done on the ship and fresh water was inadvertently run through the heads (toilets) instead of salt water. There never was an apology. Another day or two passed when one of the navy officers noticed the pennant and its case were no longer on the bulkhead; the hooks and a dark spot was all that was left. The captain went into orbit, demanding that the case and pennant be returned immediately.

Several days later, the navy challenged the pilots to a volleyball game—a huge mistake. They should have looked us over more closely. When we ran out onto the court, our little guy was six foot one; the rest of us were between six foot three and six foot five feet tall. The contest wasn't even close. To add injury to insult, one of the navy players received a spiked ball squarely in the face, resulting in a very bloody nose (I believe the spikier was a tall fellow from Michigan). The cheers of several hundred marines could only be described as raucous; I almost felt bad for the guy, but I got over it quickly.

We had a practice amphibious assault, and some liberty and returned to the ship. Shortly thereafter, our squadron mascot, a large stuffed tiger, went missing and there was a break-in of the ship's store and the armory—several watches and couple of pistols were stolen. The captain was on the speaker again, assuming that the break-ins were committed by marines as he stated, "We didn't have all this trouble before you marines came aboard!"

A week or two later, we were in Barbados for a few days of liberty. One night a landing craft full of sailors and a few marines was heading out to the ship anchored in the harbor. After a day of a sightseeing, beach-going, and probably a bit of drinking, three drunk sailors thought that it would be a good idea to throw a marine over the side into the harbor. It was not a good idea, and they certainly grabbed the wrong marine. He was a member of the Pathfinders, a reconnaissance platoon. Recon marines are considered to be the toughest of the tough, and this Marine was no exception. Before anyone could react, one sailor was in the harbor (he was retrieved), and two were unconscious on the deck of the landing craft. The executive officer of the ship wanted the marine punished. Fortunately, several of the sailors who witnessed the action said the marine was only defending himself, and that incident was forgotten.

We spent some time training in Panama. I was the squadron's escape, evasion, and survival officer, so someone who outranked me decided it would be a good idea for me to spend several days running through the jungle with the recon marines. Our job was to attack the infantry battalion, simulating guerilla attacks. I enjoyed the north woods of Michigan, Wisconsin, and Minnesota, but jungles are a different matter entirely. There are way too many creepy-crawlers, poisonous snakes, and even dangerous plants for my liking. In spite of all these things, it was a great experience working with the Pathfinders. The platoon commander was killed in Vietnam within the year.

We spent a considerable amount of time training on the island of Vieques (just east of Puerto Rico). I'm sure it was as much of a relief to the navy to have us off the ship as it was for us to be away from the navy. Without the navy to hassle, the marines turned on each other. For some time, the five or six captains in our squadron had been treating lieutenants with less than brotherly affection. They didn't eat at a table with lieutenants; they held their own parties and avoided other social functions because the lieutenants weren't "real people."

On Vieques, living conditions were rather primitive; we slept on cots in a large chicken coupe-type building and had a bathhouse that had showers but no flush toilets. The captains would not allow the lieutenants into the bathhouse when they were inside. One of the lieutenants (from a northern state) noticed that there was a fifty-five gallon drum under the roof to collect rain water. In the subtropical climate, the half-filled drum had become a home for a large number of tiny creatures living among the green, slimy growth. A plan suddenly came together, and the drum was lifted onto the roof of the bathhouse and a smoke grenade went off inside the shower area. As the naked captains came coughing out of the bathhouse, the creature-laden slime was poured over them. The timing couldn't have been worse. The colonel came around the corner of a building just in time to see the entire spectacle; he wasn't happy. That evening, there was a meeting in which we were all read the riot act. He blamed the captains for starting it and the lieutenants for finishing it. The captains paid the highest price. They had to pay for a squadron party at a club in San Juan, Puerto Rico, the following week.

Back aboard ship and heading back to North Carolina, the captain was still livid about the missing commissioning pennant. The final minutes of our time aboard the ship were at hand. Two helos remained on the flight deck to pick up the last of our maintenance personnel; I was piloting one and our executive officer the other. The captain of the ship came on the radio, "Major, if you marines don't return our commissioning pennant, I'm going to tell CINCLANTFLT (Commander in Chief of the Atlantic Fleet)." The way he said it reminded me of a little kid threatening to tell his mother about something his sibling did. The major responded, "Captain, if you sailors don't return our kitty (not the exact word he used), we're going to tell the Commandant." With that, we flew off. I gave control of the helo to my copilot. I find it hard to fly with tears in my eyes.

At the base a little later, we were greeting friends and family near the control tower. At that time, our kitty came flying by at the end of a fifty-foot rope under one of the two heavy helicopters attached to our squadron for the cruise. The captain in charge of the two heavies had our tiger the whole time. Two days later, there was a message from the CINCLANTFLT down through the chain of command ordering the colonel to conduct an investigation concerning the disappearance of the ships commissioning pennant. Each member of the squadron was ordered to report to the colonel's office as part of the investigation. Although the questioning by the colonel was tedious, grueling, and exhaustive; I remember it perfectly to this day. Upon being ordered to the CO's office, one would stand at the bulkhead adjacent to the door. One would then step forward to the center of the doorframe, do a right face to stand squarely in the doorframe. One then knocked three times. The colonel would then say. "Enter!".

At that point, one would march smartly up to eighteen inches in front of the colonel's desk, stand at attention, and eyes straight ahead, fixed on the bulkhead behind the colonel's desk.

"Sir, Lieutenant Jansen reporting as ordered!"

"Ran, do you know anything about the missing commissioning pennant?"

"No, Sir",

"Thank you. Dismissed."

"Aye, Sir".

At that point, one would take one step back, do an about face, and stride smartly out of the room. In a matter of an hour, the exhaustive investigation was over. I would have liked to have seen the message that went back up the chain of command, but I have never heard another word about it. No, I really don't know! However, I wouldn't be too surprised if the pennant could be found in a family room in Texas. The case is probably at the bottom of the Caribbean Sea.

Later the same day, I was told the colonel wanted to see me. Before I could even knock on the door, the colonel was out of his chair and greeted me warmly. He thanked me for my service with him and told me to check out of the squadron because I was going to HMM-263 the next day. The next time I would see the colonel was when he walked into my room at the Portsmouth Naval Hospital in Virginia. I had just had my fourth and final surgery on my shoulder. The date was December 1969, a little over four and a half years since I had seen him last.

The next day, I checked into HMM-263. The colonel welcomed me aboard and said that he was glad to have me; he was another fine CO. All the Marine COs I had I respected and admired, they were excellent leaders who looked after their people. If any one of the nine commanding officers I served under had told me to fly to North Vietnam and drop a dead skunk and a hand grenade down Ho Chi Minh's chimney, I would have done it. The leadership I saw in the Marine Corps was the best I have seen anywhere. In fact, I haven't seen anything even close anywhere else.

The CO of HMM-263 told me to take the rest of the week off and report in on the following Monday. By this time we heard that the unit replacing us in the Caribbean had already taken casualties in fighting in the Dominican Republic. If necessary, HMM-263 was to join them. I went to Camp LeJeune across the river and was browsing the PX (base department store) for the latest in guns and fishing tackle. While I was there, it was announced over the public address system that all marines of a certain battalion were directed to report to their areas. I dashed back to New River; I knew that if the battalion was ordered up, our squadron was also likely to go.

My new CO told me that I could stay at New River—I didn't have to go. There was no way I was going to miss any action. I told him I wanted to go. The next day, a carrier came by North Carolina to load the marine battalion and our squadron. I was one of only two pilots current for night carrier landings so the other pilot and I flew the last two helos aboard the carrier about 2200 (10 p.m.) on Saturday night. Generally, it was a very boring few weeks we spent there. For one pilot, it was not boring; he was seriously wounded but not permanently damaged. I flew 20 missions and never took a hit.

After a few weeks back in North Carolina, I took leave, went back to my family in Michigan, and then flew to Pensacola for a few days before traveling to the

Far East. I stayed with the pastor of the Presbyterian Church I had attended while in flight school. I also dated Diane a few times. This would be the last time we would see each other for nearly a year. From there, I flew to Travis Air Force Base in California. I was a member of the advance party for our squadron and flew from Travis to Japan by way of Alaska. After a day or two in Japan, we flew to Okinawa to prepare for our squadron's arrival.

The first Sunday there, I met the chaplain, and we became golfing buddies. One of the requirements to play at the nearby Kadena AFB was that one hired a local caddy. The caddies were four-and-a-half to five-feet-tall Okinawan girls. On one of the holes on the front nine, we had to walk up a rather steep hill. By this time, I was already feeling a bit uneasy about a six-foot-four, two-hundred-pound marine having his golf bag carried by a five-foot-nothing little girl. I reached over to grab the bag by the handle to take some weight off the little girl's shoulder. She turned on me like a wildcat! I threw both my arms into the air and said sorry. I have no idea what she said, but the last time I was lit into like that I was in boot camp.

For the six weeks before we went to Vietnam, we flew, played golf, and I worked on martial arts in the gymnasium. We got the call to go to Vietnam in October.

FIVE

We left Okinawa late at night and arrived in Da Nang at five in the morning—a rather ominous arrival as far as I was concerned. As I walked off the ramp of the C-130, a light, misty rain was seeping down, and I heard the booming of outgoing artillery. The first thing I saw in Vietnam was an H-34 helicopter (the type I had spent the last twenty-two months flying) parked on the ramp. It was riddled by bullets. The instant I laid eyes on it, I knew without a doubt that I was going to get hurt.

Well, we all get hurt. One cannot get through life without getting hurt. Accidents, broken relationships, sickness, loss, missteps/mistakes are all apart of life in this broken world. The point is, how are we going to deal with them? We all are in a war of some sort. As I write this in 2013, we are in a shooting war, a culture war, and a continuing spiritual battle between the flesh and the spirit. There is only one thing to do: put on the proper attitude and get on with it. I believed that God would never leave me, or forsake me. He has all knowledge and all power. Why worry? Just do your job. I put the ominous feelings out of my mind and didn't remember it again until I was on the USS *Repose*. John

Q. Adams said it well: "Duty is ours, results are God's." No matter one's occupation or life situation, this is a good thing to keep in mind.

Later that day, we were filling sandbags and digging bunkers alongside our tent at Marble Mountain, a helicopter base on the South China Sea. Within a day or two, the great shakeup came about. In order to avoid all the pilots of a squadron going home at the same time—a date based upon one's arrival over seas—it was decided all of us newcomers would be spread throughout all the Marine H-34 squadrons in Vietnam. I wound up in HMM-363 in Quin Yon. A large portion of our work was with the South Korean infantry division. I flew my first combat mission on October 13, 1965. A lot of the flying was boring such as hauling food and water to outposts. A lot of it was difficult, like landing on the side of a steep hill or hovering over small openings in the jungle, sometimes even in the middle of the night.

Our living quarters ("hooches") were sandbagged but were only a hand-grenade-throw from a fence that separated us from whomever in the town of Quin Yon. I wasn't happy about this, so I volunteered to be the officer of the guard every third night. I hoped that if we were attacked, it would be on my night so I could meet it head-on without having to try to find a hole in the ground while half asleep. In the couple of months we were there, we were not attacked.

In early January of 1966, we moved up to Chu Lai to join the other squadrons in our air group. My helicopter was hit by ground fire only a couple of times while operating at Quin Yon. Now things were getting hot—instead of getting a bullet in the tail section once in a while, the bullets were often coming through the cockpit.

February 23 marked a wild mission. I was flying as copilot as we wound our way up a rain-shrouded valley. Our mission was to extract a group of recon marines. Before we had gone very far, bullets began ripping through the helicopter. Because of the damage reported by the crew chief down below, the pilot decided we couldn't make it to our destination and back, so he decided to turn back and go by a different way after getting an undamaged helicopter at the base. As he rolled out of the steep turn and leveled off, we took a direct hit from the front. A flame shot up in front of me, and as I looked down, I saw some blood seeping out of my flight suit and felt numbness from the waist down. The helicopter was a little more difficult to control but still flying with the engine running just fine. I grabbed the fire extinguisher, but the fire was just an electrical fire and died instantly. We were busy flying the wounded bird, but the thought went through my mind that we might not make it out of this valley. We could die in a crash, be forced to land, and have to fight our way out of the shooting gallery we were in or get captured. No matter what happened, I knew my life was God's, and the final result was in his hands.

A few minutes later, we were in a safer area, and I began to asses the situation. Our primary flight instruments were off, as were all the electronics and communication and navigation radios. The automatic stabilization equipment, which helps in controlling a helicopter, was also off. I could see a hole in the floor just forward of my right rudder pedal. The bullet had come up from the bottom, through the cockpit floor, and through a large bundle of wires. The shock of the bullet on the floor is what apparently gave me the numb feeling in my legs. As I cocked my head a little, I could see the hole the bullet made coming through the cockpit floor was right in line with my upper chest and head. *Where did that bullet go?* I wondered. Then I noticed it had hit my rudder pedal and had blown up. The main part of the bullet hit my shin but was stopped by maps in the pocket of my flight suit. Pieces of the floor, wiring, and pieces of the bullet had punctured the upper portion of my inner thighs. If that bullet had been 5/8 of an inch either forward or back, it would have hit me square in the upper chest or head. Months later, some pieces of wire worked their way out of my upper thighs.

Here is the bottom line that we all have to think about:—no matter how well trained, no matter how smart, no matter how much knowledge we have, no matter how hard we work, study, or think, God has a final say in everything. We were traveling at 100 mph, the bullet was doing in excess of 2000 fps, yet 5/8 of an inch either way would probably have killed me. I wound up with a few stitches, a few band-aids, and a tetanus shot. Do everything you can, trust God, and live and learn from the consequences.

Ten days later, I was piloting a helicopter in a flight of sixteen, each chopper with a crew of four and probably six to eight marines aboard, one bullet hit that entire formation. It came within an inch or two of my crew chiefs head and hit the bottom of my seat a quarter of an inch from the edge. The bullet splattered, some going into the control panel and the rest going into my left calf and ankle. Again, we were doing 100 mph, the bullet 2000 fps. If that bullet had been 1/4 an inch further back, it would have entered my right buttock and traveled through my heart and lungs. I picked up a rather uncomplimentary nickname: Old Magnet Elbow, or something like that.

By late March, our squadron had lost two pilots and the crew chief and gunner. The helicopter was shot down, killing the four crew members and all the marine passengers. Several other pilots had been wounded.

There were many missions. Overall I flew 248 in the seven months I served in Vietnam. One other mission convinced me of the absolute sovereignty of God. I was flying wing in a two helicopter re-supply/ medical evacuation mission. We again had to fly low, up a valley to avoid fire from the top of the hills. Both helicopters landed, unloaded ammunition, food and water, and took on some wounded marines. We lifted up, did a turn on the spot, and I led out, again flying low and taking a different path out of the area. We came to an area that was less wooded, which gave the enemy a greater chance to get a shot off at us. I began to feel a bit uneasy. I pulled back on the cyclic stick, putting us into a climb. In that nanosecond, two bullets hit us from the front—one under me, the other under my copilot. At the same time, a machine gun hit us from the side. If I had not pulled up the second I did, I believe both of us would have been hit, and the machine gun would have killed most of the marines in the passenger compartment. The lesson: give your life to God, work like it all depends on you, and pray like it all depends on him. We have no way of knowing what is coming our way, accidents, sickness, or any of the multitude of problems we face on this fallen planet. He guides us, he influences our thoughts, he has the final word. He is trustworthy. I was a well trained, skilled, highly experienced combat pilot flying a well designed, built and maintained helicopter. That had nothing to do with the outcome—it was 100 % grace of a sovereign God.

My turn came for R & R (rest and relaxation), and I was sent to Hong Kong for four days. A good bed with sheets, a real bathroom, and good food was a real treat to say the least. I met another marine lieutenant on the plane. We hit it off and discovered neither of us were into drinking or debauchery, so we did the Hong Kong tour together. The final day we dined on the floating restaurant in the bay. While we dined in luxury, a short distance away was abject poverty. A hill within our sight was covered with flimsy boxes and shacks as shelter for those escaping Red China. The bay was packed with narrow boats side by side with planks running across their sterns. One would have to cross many boats to get to his own boat in the middle of the pack. Children swam in the filthy water.

I am continually amazed at the amount of poverty and suffering throughout the world. Another thing that astounds me is this: Americans are the most wealthy, prosperous, and free people on earth, yet they complain continually. Even the poor in America are better off than a large portion of the world's population. It seems we are never satisfied. There is always a new fishing rod, set of golf clubs, car, clothes, or house that we have our hearts set on.

I managed to get a phone call through to Pensacola, Florida, to my unofficial fiancée. Diane told me about her upcoming visit to my family in Michigan the following week. We also discussed getting married when I got home. Little did I know that I would be seeing her in less than three weeks. I returned to Vietnam on the 27th of April, flew on the 28th, and got shot the final time on April 29th.

SIX

The ninth floor of the naval hospital at the Great Lakes Naval Training Center was my new home. The care was great, even though perhaps it was a little over done. There were many navy corpsmen in training at the hospital, so we had our blood pressure and our temperature taken often along with many questions as to how we were doing. The entire staff was great!

The next day, as I was walking down the hallway, I found myself face to face with my parents, brother and sister, and Diane who had just gotten off the elevator. A few hours later, we were all in the car heading to Holland, Michigan. Several days later, my fiancée flew back to Florida to plan our wedding, which would take place on July 16, 1966. I spent the next seven weeks going back and forth from Holland to the naval hospital. Therapy was the least amount of fun I had in years, struggling to get the muscles working again was difficult at best. The good news was that the doctor at the Great Lakes hospital was more optimistic about the range of motion I could expect.

A week before our wedding date, I flew to Pensacola, Florida, beating an airline strike by a day. Upon arriving in Florida, I discovered Diane's car was a little Corvair which did not accommodate my six-foot-four frame. We took it down to the local Pontiac dealer and traded it in for a '66 Pontiac Catalina.

Prior to my arriving in Florida, Diane had called a marine friend, Captain Ed Meixner, who was instructing in flight school. Captain Meixner and I had been together on the Mediterranean cruise two years earlier. He would be my best man and was asked to round up a few more marines as groomsmen (Ed was killed in Vietnam in 1968). The wedding was conducted by Don Patterson of the Presbyterian Church where I had attended during flight school.

Our brief honeymoon was in Alabama at a resort on the Mobile Bay. Several days later, we loaded Diane's possessions into the Pontiac and headed to Holland for another wedding reception with my family. The next six weeks were spent mainly in Holland with weekly trips to the hospital for therapy. This got old in a hurry, and Diane suggested that perhaps we could be sent to a marine base where I could get therapy and hold down a desk job while on limited duty. The doctor agreed and notified the marine barracks at Great Lakes to request orders from marine headquarters in Washington, DC to order me to limited duty.

A few days later, I received orders to report to the Second Marine Aircraft Wing at MCAS Cherry Point, North Carolina, which was the home of the Second Wing's fighter and transport aircraft. Somehow, somewhere, the word *limited* was left out of my orders. Far be it for me to say anything, I was ready to fly in spite of the seriously limited mobility of my left arm.

I walked into the wing personnel office where I was greeted by an unhappy major who wanted to know what the —— I was doing there. Evidently, somewhere along the line, I was supposed to have received a supplement to my orders directing me to the helicopter base at MCAF New River, some sixty miles away. He wanted to know what he should do with me. I was happy to tell him that I would rather be the shooter than the shootee, and therefore would like to be assigned to a fighter squadron so I could return to Vietnam and chase Russian MiGs and drop big bombs on the bad guys. "F-4 Phantoms would be fine with me, if you don't mind, sir."

"Come back in a half an hour. I'll see what I can do," he said in a much quieter attitude. I had seen him glance at my ribbons, and I guess seeing my Purple Heart made him think I had had enough of helicopters. A half hour later, I found out that I was going to the fighter training squadron on our base.

I checked into the squadron, and although I had not yet gotten into a jet, I was flying high! The next day, my wife and the CO pinned captain bars on my collar. My date of rank was August 3, 1966. Now I was really flying high—a beautiful new bride, new captain bars, three rows of ribbons, and I was in a jet squadron. Wow! The crash was immanent. Later that day, I met the squadron flight surgeon and received my annual flight physical. I passed everything until I got to the point where a fighter pilot is required to put both hands over his head to reach the ejection handle above and behind his head.

My left hand nearly got to my face. "You are not flying until you can reach the handle," he told me.

The next two weeks I worked as adjutant (administrative assistant to the CO) and tried to force my left arm higher and higher. By this time, it was late September 1966. The war in Vietnam was ratcheting up and more pilots were needed. The commanding general of the wing called the squadron leaders and senior wing officers together. One of the things he wanted to know was if there were pilots anywhere in the wing whose primary job was not flying. He was told of a Captain Jansen who was an adjutant. The general wanted to know why said captain was not flying. He was told the captain could not reach the ejection seat handle. The general then told the personnel officer to send the captain's elbow to the C-130 squadron because C-130s did not have ejection seats.

Imagine with me for a moment. Suppose your father had told you that in a few weeks, he would give you the keys to a hot sports car. A few weeks pass, and he calls you in and says that he is sorry but due to circumstances, he cannot give you the sports car; however, he does have an old beat-up pickup truck you can have instead.

The disappointment that slammed me was like being told by the doctor aboard the *Repose* that my career was over. Again, in spite of the crushing disappointment, I figured God had a hand in this, and I would go on and do my duty. The C-130 is a great airplane, but we didn't chase MiGs or drop bombs out of it. We hauled people, equipment, supplies, and refueled fighters in the air. For the most part, it was many hours of boredom as we flew all over North America, Central America, and to Europe.

Diane and I settled into our apartment on the base, and we got involved with squadron activities and with a church nearby. My golf clubs arrived from the Far East, and I got into the swing again, although with a decidedly different swing due to my seriously damaged left arm and shoulder. I was happily married, grateful to be alive, and associating with a great bunch of marines. But it was difficult to be living the good life with my American brothers dying daily on the other side of the world. It was difficult not to be involved directly in the war—a feeling I still have to this day.

Flying has been defined as hours and hours of boredom interrupted by moments of stark terror—this really applies to flying transport planes. The C-130 was and still is a great, dependable plane, but the flying was generally boring. There were moments, however. One night we were taking a load of marines and radar vehicles to Iceland, cruising along at about thirty thousand feet. Except for the red glow of the instrument panel, the cockpit is dark. We were lounging in our huge seats, monitoring the instruments, totally relaxed, and talking about nothing important on the intercom. There is nothing to see outside the aircraft except blackness. Suddenly, three things took place simultaneously: the instrument panel lit up like a Christmas tree, the aircraft went into a climb, and all four engines were surging a percent or two. The first thing a pilot needs to do in an emergency is fly the plane; pilots have crashed because they became overly absorbed in the problem and failed to fly the plane. I was in the left seat (aircraft commander seat), so I grabbed the controls and returned the aircraft to our assigned altitude while the flight engineer and the other pilot tried to find out what went wrong.

Each of the four engines has a generator to produce electrical power, and each has its own electrical bus that it powers. Normally, when a generator quit, the electrical load automatically went to another engine. The pilot would never know he had lost a generator until told by the flight engineer who monitored the generators. We had lost a generator and the automatic switch did not function. The generator that quit carried power to the warning light system, the automatic pilot, and the engine syncrophaser. We had burned off thousands of pounds of fuel, which caused the aircraft to go into a steep climb. Because the syncrophazer had gone off, all the engines were trying to slave to a master engine, which caused a change in the RPM.

In this case, we had to shut down the engine with the faulty generator. Flying a C-130 with three engines is fine, but we still had another problem, which for a while made us think we had to shut down another engine. Fortunately, it all worked out, and we landed in Iceland on three engines. Those few minutes were not stark terror, but it definitely got our attention.

There is an old story line pilots like to use when telling of a flying incident: "There I was fat, dumb, and happy when suddenly—" Life is like that—all is fine until something happens unexpectedly. The main thing is to keep on flying.

Another time, I was training a new C-130 pilot. He had just made a short field landing, where we landed with full flaps at the lowest possible speed. As soon as the aircraft touches down, all four engines are put into full reverse (which is up to 60 percent of total engine power), and the brakes are applied full force. We dropped off a marine passenger and returned to the end of the runway to do a short field takeoff. The engines are run to full power while the brakes hold the aircraft in position. The brakes are released and as soon as flight speed is attained, the nose is pulled up, wheels retracted, and the climb out is conducted at maximum nose up attitude. At this time, one engine just quit. We had just enough altitude to push the nose over and stay above the trees. Had we been heavy, or if the engine had quit a second or two earlier, I don't know if we would have made it.

Another emergency occurred while we were aerial refueling fighters off the East Coast. One of the fighter pilots notified us that we were leaking fuel out of our left wing. We shut down the engine near the leek and headed for the base. I declared an emergency and landed at Cherry Point with no flaps and no brakes to avoid any sparks that would set off the leaking fuel. It was a little unnerving to be chased down the runway by fire trucks, but to reiterate an old pilot's saying, "We didn't hurt nobody and didn't break nuthin'."

By the middle of 1968, my shoulder was giving me a lot of trouble. There was always a certain amount of pain and sometimes it felt like it was beginning to dislocate. I didn't want to say anything because I was scheduled to return to the Far East by April of 1969. At that time, I hoped to transfer to the new Cobra gun ships the Marine Corps was utilizing in Vietnam. C-130 flying was just too boring for me; I wanted to get back into the action.

In January 1969, I took a C-130 with a copilot in-training to Lajes AFB in the Azores. As we approached the base, we were in instrument flight rules with severe turbulence. It was pitch dark and raining heavily. We were on a GCA (Ground Controlled Approach), where the radar operator on the ground tells the pilot whether he is on glide slope, above or below, or left or right of the invisible radar beam. Just before we reached field minimums (125 feet above the ground and a quarter of a mile from the end of the runway), my left shoulder felt like it was coming apart. At that time, I could flex my upper arm and shoulder to get it back into position. Fortunately, it popped back in because I did not want to turn the plane over to an inexperienced copilot in that situation. The GCA operator called me at field minimums, which means that the pilot must either take over visually, or if he cannot see the runway, he must go to another airport or try another pass. I decided that this aircraft was going to be landed because there was no place else to go, and I was not going to go around through that turbulence again. The operator kept on giving us information as to our position on the glide scope. He called me at fifty feet above the runway. The copilot asked if the runway lights were on; the operator replied they were on full intensity. At twenty-five feet, I could still see nothing.

The pilot's job is to hold the landing attitude and maintain the correct airspeed. About the time I picked up the glimmer of lights, the aircraft touched down.

The next day, Sunday, the copilot flew us back to North Carolina. Monday morning I went to my flight surgeon and grounded myself. He took me to see two orthopedic surgeons visiting from Portsmouth, Virginia. I was standing behind the two doctors as they looked at my X-rays. "What have you been doing?" one asked. "I've been flying C-130s," I responded. *"You've been what?"* he yelled back. He then proceeded to chew me out like the girl caddy in Okinawa—only this time I understood what was being said. He informed me that my shoulder needed to be fused and that would be the end of me in the Marine Corps.

I had surgery in March of 1969. After four months in a body cast, the procedure failed and surgery was repeated in December with a new technique and three more months in a body cast. Fishing and golfing in a body cast was not easy, but it helped pass the time. This time the surgery was successful. I had to appear before a medical board which told me I would be forced to retire at 30 percent disability. After nine years in the corps, a new chapter of my life was about to begin. There was some inner peace, and I knew God wasn't surprised by any of this, but I was not happy.

SEVEN

July 31, 1970, was my last day in the Marine Corps. VMGR-252 (the C-130 squadron) at Cherry Point had a retirement ceremony for several marines. We each received a handshake from the colonel and a letter from the commandant of the corps thanking us for our service. Each of the other marines, being retired, had twenty or more years of service, so there was plenty of handshaking, backslapping, and laughing as members of the squadron bid them farewell.

I didn't hang around; I left my wife in the company of the colonel and several of the wives as I walked alone out to the flight line among the aircraft. I didn't want to see or talk to anybody. I had served nine years and twenty-eight days. Since everyone knew that I was sick about being forced to retire, they wisely left me alone. That night, there was a squadron party at the officer's club, and we received well wishes from all the members. After the party, we stayed with friends. All of our belongings were on a moving van headed toward Holland, Michigan. Saturday morning, the first of August, Diane, myself, twenty-eight-month-old Theresa, our German shepherd, with my fishing boat in tow, left North Carolina for Michigan.

As we settled into a rented house, I was not a happy camper, even though I still had a sense of inner peace and comfort in knowing God had not left us. I had little, if any, direction as to what work I wanted to do. Life outside the corps had a definite lack of adventure and excitement. Beside my family and the good fishing in Michigan, I wasn't interested in much. I entered college in September with the intention of becoming a school teacher, but my heart wasn't in it.

After a year of school, my grades had gone from excellent to passing. During the third trimester, we had the blessing of our second child, Craig, in April of 1971. There were a few things I was happy about, which were my family, fishing, and the fact that I wasn't in jail. There were several times I wanted to do some serious bodily harm to the war protesters on campus. One day, as I was walking down a corridor in one of the campus buildings, I heard some loud cheering going on in an auditorium. As I looked in through a partially opened door, I saw on a movie screen an F-8 Crusader jet flown by the Navy and Marine Corps, going down in flames over Vietnam. I had friends who flew F-8s. As I pondered going into the auditorium and busting some heads and equipment, I decided that going to jail and paying damages wasn't worth it. I went home and didn't go back very often.

I spent a lot of time with my growing, young family, worked part time at temporary jobs, fished, and to my surprise and delight, I began playing golf again. After my last surgery in December 1969, the doctors told me that I would not be able to play golf; my upper left arm had been fused permanently to the shoulder blade, which seriously limited mobility. I sold my clubs before leaving the corps.

In January of 1971, we were visiting my parents, and my dad had his golf clubs out in preparation for a Florida vacation. I picked up a club and made a short, abbreviated swing. My dad took one look and said we should see what I could do swinging at a real ball. It happened to be Wednesday night, and the local civic center had a golf net set up as an indoor driving range. Obviously, we couldn't tell too much about the flight of the ball, but Dad said it sounded like I was hitting it pretty hard.

Two months later, when the snow was gone, I went to a local country club and told the pro my story. He gave me a couple of golf balls, loaned me a set of used clubs, and told me to go see what I could do—no charge. I shot nine over par for nine holes after not hitting a golf ball for over two years. I bought the clubs and have been playing ever since.

In January of 1972, I began an eighteen-month job as a community recreation director, which was federally funded to ease the high unemployment rate in Michigan. I developed a community-wide program using school facilities along with planning a park. Following that, I was back to part-time temporary jobs, which did not help my overall attitude. I was extremely hostile. My hostility was directed at the media which had been grossly slanting and misrepresenting the war news, the politicians who mishandled the war, the protesters who gave great encouragement and comfort to the enemy, and my government which I believed was short-changing me. My anger was eating me up. Finally, I came to my senses and told the Lord that I forgave them all. The sense of peace and comfort was overwhelming. I realized that I had done more to God than anyone had ever done to me. He forgave me, how could I possibly not forgive others?

Late one sleepless night, I had another brief chat with the Lord, basically telling him that I had done pretty much of what I wanted to do during my life so far. From now on, I would do whatever he wanted, wherever he wanted me to do it. Immediately, an overwhelming sense of peace came over me, and I simply passed out. The next morning when I awoke, I wondered for a moment what had happened. Had that been a dream? However, I repeated my new commitment. I expected the phone to ring and for someone to say that I was needed to fly missionary airplanes in Africa. For a moment, I felt a little sad because now that I had made this new commitment, I figured that this would be the end of my canoe/fishing trips to Canada and a lot of my other fun stuff. I had always believed that once you committed your life to the Lord, your fun was over. This idea is, of course, nonsense. Much to my surprise, absolutely nothing happened! I still had no direction and no job. The ways in which the Lord took care of us are too many to relate here, but I'll mention a couple things. One of the things I learned is that he takes us through many difficult things, which we don't always understand at the time, but our experiences are designed for developing character and commitment to him.

The Marine Corps knows how to take a punk kid and turn him into the world's finest fighter. God certainly knows even better how to take a fallen sinner and turn him into his own likeness to accomplish his work in his time and place. There is an expression applicable to the corps and God's army: "No pain, no gain."

I had signed up with a temporary job service in our area and had a job beginning on a Monday morning unloading trucks. We needed fifty dollars by that Friday, so I called the office to see if I could be paid by then. The answer was no. That afternoon, I had to unload frozen food from a railcar, which required overhead lifting. With a left hand that couldn't get above my face, I was having a hard time, and this was the only job they had for me. On the way home, I informed the Lord that I was thankful for the work I had, but I still needed fifty dollars by Friday and unless he healed my shoulder, I wouldn't be able to continue with the job at the warehouse. Ten minutes after I got home, there was a phone call from out of the blue. A friend who owned a sporting goods store called to ask me if I was available for two weeks to fill in as a clerk. The next morning, he showed me how to run the cash register (I knew where everything was in the store) and asked if I had any questions. I asked when payday was. He opened his wallet and gave me a hundred dollars in advance.

Two weeks later, I was heading home after work. I thanked the Lord for the work and asked about what was next. I found out ten minutes after I got home—two months of running the club house at a local golf course. About a week before this job was to terminate (the golf course owner's son was coming home from college to take over), I got a call from a guy from church who was a probation officer. He told me to contact the chief probation officer for our county. The chief said that they had received federal funds to take some hard-core juvenile delinquents on a rigorous, outdoor adventure. He wanted to know if I was interested in leading the group.

That June, I had a local police officer and four teenagers in my station wagon headed for Canada for a two-week canoe trip. The four teenagers came from broken and dysfunctional homes, one had been picked up for drunk and disorderly conduct at the age of eleven, another of the boys had over one hundred arrests for breaking and entering.

The first day into the wilderness it rained most of the day. The boys were extremely nervous about eating that night because we had no stoves and were to cook over an open fire. I assured them that there was plenty of dry wood in the forest. Late that afternoon, we set up camp by a beautiful waterfall. I took the boys into the woods and helped them to get the dry wood from under deadfalls. Only one of the boys wanted to fish, so I took him out in a canoe below the waterfall. He soon hooked a three-foot-long Northern Pike; he was excited to say the least. He asked if I would clean it and cook it for him. I said "No, you are going to do it." At that point, he protested that he didn't know how. I told him that he could do it; I would talk him through it. He did clean it, cook it, and was exuberant over the experience. I have never seen such a look of triumph and accomplishment on a kid's face before or since. From that time on, he took in every word the cop and I said. The last I heard, he wanted to become a police officer.

There was another kid on that trip we'll call Joe (I called him a lot of things under my breath), a more obnoxious person I have never met. By the end of the first day, I was contemplating three courses of action: (1) drown him, (2) feed him to the bears, or (3) drown him and then feed him to the bears. I realized that this could cause some tough questions if I returned with three instead of four. By the second day, there were some changes in Joe's behavior. By the third day, I was no longer contemplating the three courses of action and was relieved that I wouldn't have to answer any tough questions about returning home minus one. On the fifth day, Joe was sitting in the canoe just in front of me. I said "Joe, what have you learned on this trip?" He replied, "I learned that I have been a real jerk to my mother and sister." I about fell out of the canoe.

A week after our return, I got a call from the chief probation officer. He said that Joe's probation officer had never seen a bigger change in a kid in such a short time. He also asked me if I would take another group of kids in August. To make a long story short, I wound up taking two groups of troubled teenagers on camping/canoeing/fishing trips to Canada. These were not the usual fun trips I had before, but these two trips were very rewarding, and I was paid to go fishing. This type of provision was not unique during the period of time from my retirement until now. One of the major lessons

I learned through all of this was that we should always be thankful in all circumstances, praising God because he is always at work in us to develop character and bring us to maturity. Getting what we wanted would lead us to selfishness and away from God's kingdom. Duty is ours, results are God's.

It is common in some areas of Christianity to believe that if one comes to God that God will bless that person with unlimited health, blessings, and prosperity. Baloney! God said that in this life, there will be trouble and persecution—if Jesus had trouble, so will we. Jesus said a servant is not higher than his master. He is not our servant to get us what we want. We are at war. Yes, he does give us blessings of peace and joy; he provides, but we are here to occupy (fight the battle) until he comes back.

Another problem I see is that many Christians blame the devil for everything in their lives they don't like or they think is bad. The devil is not omniscient or omnipresent—he has been defeated by Jesus and nothing gets to us unless it comes through God. Yes, by not following God's Word and by committing sins, we can get ourselves into a mess, but even that God works out for the best if we will repent and follow his ways. God is in the business of training people to be effective in his army, not to see how easy he can make it for us.

Another thing while I'm at it: God isn't always going to make it clear what he is up to in our lives—this is where faith and trust come in. Do your job, follow his ways, trust him, praise him, and he will take care of the results. Get to know him, commit to him. Yes, there is a cost to following God in this life, but the cost of not following him is totally unacceptable.

By 1975, I was still basically unemployed and not sure of what I should or could do. That spring, we began to hear about Christ for the Nations Institute, a Bible school in Dallas, Texas. On May 28, 1975, we had been accepted and decided we would sell everything and move to Dallas. The next day, our seven-year-old daughter, Theresa, was hit by a car doing 35–40 mph. Following school that day, she had gone to a classmate's home located on a busy road between the beach and the town. We had told her not to cross that road. Evidentially, the girls had seen something across the road and went to check it out. We could only guess what went through her mind because the only recollection of that entire day she had was eating berries and whipped cream before they went outside. She probably remembered that we had told her not to cross the road, and she suddenly darted back across into the path of a car. From that point on, there was a series of God-involved events. The father of the little girl she had gone home with saw the accident. First, he was hemophobic; he could not even deal with a child's bloody nose. Second, he was not able to get onto his knees due to surgery, and third, he had been told never to touch an accident victim. He rushed out to our daughter who was covered in blood. He dropped to his knees on the road and slapped her on the back, which forced blood out of her mouth, and she began breathing.

Theresa was unconscious for six days and then began a rapid recovery, including a miraculous lengthening and straightening of her leg. She had been limping badly and had been using a walker. One day, the pastor called her to the front of the church and prayed for her. I carried the walker out of our church, and she was walking without a limp. The doctor had said she would be limping for a couple of years. Today she has earned two master's degrees and is a college professor.

Instead of going to Dallas in the fall of 1975, we moved in January 1976 and left our home on the market. Bible school was the next big chapter in our lives.

EIGHT

Upon our arrival on the campus of Christ for the Nations in Dallas, Texas, in early January 1976, we moved into a two-bedroom apartment and were immersed into a new culture. The students ranged in ages from eighteen to the seventies and came from a wide range of backgrounds. Many different denominations were represented; there were a few retired military people and many young people fresh out of horrific lives of crime, drugs, alcohol, and prostitution.

I learned a lot at the Bible school, some of it even came from the classroom. One of the issues at school was money—most of us didn't have much. A couple of days before the end of January, we had just eaten our last morsel of food in the apartment, and we had no money; my retirement check was two or three days away. Diane and I mentioned it to the Lord, and a few seconds after we said "amen," there was a knock on the door. I opened the door to see a young student with a ten dollar bill held up to my face. "The Lord told me to give this to you," he said. I assured him that we were fine, and we didn't need it, but he insisted, so I thanked him and took it. I guess I would have felt better about it if he had been a lot older and perhaps been a captain or higher in rank. The amazing thing was that he was on his way to help us before we had even prayed. A retired marine captain being helped by a young kid—the Lord certainly has a sense of humor—and I probably could use a little (okay, a lot) of humility training.

Another money incident took place in early December, shortly before the Christmas break. Diane had been working part-time, and we had eighty dollars saved up to go to Pensacola to be with her family at Christmas. One day, I came home from school, and she informed me that she felt that the Lord wanted us to give that money away. "*What?*" One thing I had learned over the years is that women in general and my wife in particular are more sensitive to spiritual matters and peoples' needs. *Okay,* I thought, *I better ask God what he thinks about this.* I did and felt that she was right. I believe God said that there were people on campus who needed money now and that he would take care of our trip. We prayed together and came up with four couples we felt God had put on our hearts. We gave twenty dollars to each of the four couples, all of whom said that they had just prayed for money. Within a few days, we had four times what we had given away. Diane's sister unexpectedly sent us a check, my insurance company gave me an unexpected rebate, and two other sources I don't recall combined to give us the $320 dollars. There are some ministries that teach that we are to give in order to receive. I disagree. We are to give as we are blessed and as God directs; giving in order to receive isn't giving at all.

I learned another huge lesson that first semester. Before leaving for Dallas, I had worked part-time for a guy I knew in Holland. He owed me $140 dollars, but I knew he was strapped for cash, so I told him he could give me $70 dollars then, and after I got to Dallas, he could send me the rest when I sent him my address. He was very relieved and thanked me. About two weeks after we got to Dallas, I sent him a letter, gave him my address, and told him things were going well at school. Several weeks went by with no response. I sent him another letter telling him that we were enjoying school but certainly could use the $70 dollars; in those days that was a lot of money. Seventy dollars was a tank of gas, a lot of groceries, and a round of golf. Several more weeks went by—nothing. Now I was getting aggravated. I sent him yet another letter, a very nice letter—really! More weeks went by—nothing. Now I was ready to skin him alive, this was on my mind when I got up in the morning, and when I went to bed at night, I was agitated and angry. It suddenly dawned on me again that no one had ever done more to me than what I had done to Jesus—my sins put him on the cross. I wrote another letter—I told him to consider the debt paid. When I dropped the letter into the mailbox, I felt an enormous sense of relief and an overwhelming sense of peace.

That summer, we took a brief vacation to Holland. The guy heard we were in town and called the place where we were staying. He offered me a free trip to the golf course and gave me a check for $70 dollars when we were done playing. The lesson is simple: forgive everybody for everything, because God forgives us far more.

Another incident gave me a lot of insight. One day when I got home from school at noon, I had a little lunch and wondered what to do. The kids were in school, Diane was at work, and all my class work was done. Since I was in a Bible school to learn about God and how to do what he wanted, I felt that it was a good time to seek God's will and find out what he wanted me to do that afternoon. I said, "Okay, Lord. What do you want me to do this afternoon?" Instantly, I felt I heard, "Play golf." I couldn't believe it; I had to be making this up. I had no preconceived ideas as to what he might want of me, so I asked again and received the same "play golf" response. Now I was a little agitated to say the least. I was ready to do whatever he wanted of me, and he wouldn't talk to me, so how can I serve him if I can't hear his instructions?

I stewed for a few minutes—a little angry with him for not making it clear and disgusted with myself for not being able to hear him. Then the thought came: *Perhaps he does want me to play golf.* "Where?" I asked. Immediately, a golf course I didn't care about came to mind. I loaded my clubs into the car and took off, not sure of what this was all about. Fifteen minutes later, I was at the driving range at the course and began talking to another guy hitting a few shots. The conversation ended over an hour later. All I can remember was that the guy had been involved in church years before and had gotten away from it. I don't remember ten words I said, but I know I gave him the message that God wanted him to hear. I have no idea what has taken place in that man's life after that; all I know is that God wanted me to talk to him.

Here, to me anyway, is the bottom line: if we are committed to God, we do not need to be asking him what we need to do minute by minute or day by day. We are to do our jobs and take care of our responsibilities in our families, our church, and our vocations. He knows our needs, he knows when we need a break, and he is in charge of all divine appointments. God sent me to that guy only because I was available at that time and place to communicate with him. Each of us has experiences, abilities, and characteristics that God knows when, where, and how to use. Be committed to God, be available to be used; then you don't have to fret about doing—just be. He directs our paths.

In April of 1977, a month before graduation, my wife and one of our female retired military friends suggested that I go to Oral Roberts University in Tulsa. I didn't think I would be accepted because of my late application, and I really didn't want to go to school anymore, but I applied to get the girls off my back. I was accepted. In August of 1977, I began two years of school at ORU, the eighth school since I graduated from high school, all for a guy who hated school.

ORU is a great school. I'm not a fan of all of Oral Robert's teaching, but I thought very highly of all the professors I met. The facilities are outstanding, as are the students. Our kids enjoyed themselves as well; they went to athletic events and really had a good time using the gymnasium which was open on Friday nights for families only.

The last term was my favorite; all my requirements had been met, so I loaded up on sports classes. I played tennis, racquetball, basketball, korfball (Dutch basketball), baseball, team handball, rugby, weight lifting, and I got certified in scuba diving. I also played a weekly round of golf. This amounted to a four-month-long recreational recess. One day I was walking down a hallway. Under my left arm were tennis and racquetball racquets, in my left hand were swim fins, goggles, and a snorkel. In my right hand, I had a baseball bat and glove. One of my classmates approached me, shook his head, and said, "Jansen, you're just a big kid." That made my day.

I did take two real classes, one of which was on eschatology (the doctrine of "last days" or "the end of the world"). One thing I had noticed over the years is that if you want to pick a fight among Christians, all one had to do is to mention the term *end times*. There are three major views on how the end of the world will take place, and I have never seen an issue where people are more locked into a certain point of view; disagree with them, and the fight is on. I decided I was going to settle this once and for all, at least in my own mind. I was disappointed that I wasn't able to nail the whole issue down as far as finding out which of the three points of view is correct because each of them has their strong and weak points. I do, however, lean more strongly toward one view.

My experience in Vietnam settled the issue for me. *What?* Hang on, I'll make the connection. Most of the guys in Vietnam could tell you to the day when they were going home. I couldn't have told you to the nearest month when I was going to leave, I paid no attention to the matter. My goal was to do my job as best I could. The possibility of getting seriously hurt or killed was with us daily. I figured that thinking about going home would interfere with my aggressiveness and commitment to the job. I didn't want to become overly cautious as I approached the end of my tour. So this is how I settled the eschatology issue: from the a-millennial position, I get the idea of living in God's kingdom now, daily, minute by minute. He is with us, he is in us, and he has a job for us to do. Don't worry about when the job will be over, because we don't know.

From the post-millennial view, I get the idea that we should be having a significant impact on this society and the people around us; fix what is wrong, do what is right, and leave the results to God; we are to be salt and light to the world. From the pre-millennial position, I get the concept of being ready because we don't know when God is returning, it could be any minute, and we have no clue as to when we will be leaving. In this life, we can get hit by a bullet, a drunk driver, have a heart attach, or die suddenly in many other ways. Do your job and don't worry about getting out of this mess. Life is full of messes and opportunities—just get to work.

Taking things in stride and being committed to God is a way of life. God is in the business of building character and having a relationship with us. Testing and training is always an ongoing process. Enjoy his presence, his guidance, and his eternal promises. Nothing on this earth is worth striving for or hanging onto. Billy Graham said that he had never seen a hearse pulling a U-Haul. Duty is ours, results are God's.

NINE

One of the principles I had learned from my parents is that in any job we should work "as onto the Lord." In other words, we have a boss on the job, but our real boss is God. We should work every job as though God was watching, and we should work to please him. If we work as we should, God will take care of the results; sometimes we will be rewarded above and beyond what we deserve, and in other times, we may be cheated or not be recognized as we should. Leave the results with him and be thankful for whatever job we have. Duty is ours, results are God's.

While in Michigan, before leaving for Texas, I had a temporary job where I modified the procedure which resulted in a 45 percent increase in production without increasing the cost one cent, I was hoping for a nice bonus, all I got was a sincere "thank you" from the boss. The lesson is that we should always do our best; rewards may or may not be received in this life.

In my last semester at ORU, I had a job as a part-time retail sales clerk in the sporting goods department of a large department store. We were paid $2.98 per hour with a 2 percent bonus on all sales. Behind the sales room was a storage area where the merchandise was kept; this was a disaster area. Clerks didn't want to spend any time back there to keep things in order because that would reduce one's time on the sales floor. One day, I asked myself how I would act if this was God's store. From that time on, I would take a few minutes out, here and there, to restore order and safety to the merchandise room. An amazing thing happened: my sales topped all the other clerks.

One evening, things were rather quiet, the merchandise room was squared away (marine term for *orderly*), and there were a few clerks milling around. A shabbily dressed man came in and wanted to look at the rifles. The other clerks did not give him a second glance. I struck up a conversation with him; we talked rifles and shooting. I showed him a couple of the rifles he was interested in, and then he said, "I'll take that one," pointing to the most expensive rifle we had ($800). At that point, he reached into his pocket and pulled out a huge roll of money and pealed off $850, which he handed to me. Another lesson: treat everybody as somebody, regardless of what they look like or where they come from.

In July 1979, I began the most unusual of my many jobs: pastoring a small, non-denominational church in a St. Louis suburb. The church grew rapidly for two years until the split came. The problem with an independent, non-denominational church is that if issues arise, there is no place to go, no higher authority to arbitrate dissension. Those with whom we had the issue refused to discuss it with anybody else. Eighty percent of the church stayed with me. Unfortunately, we had no control over the facilities, so we wound up meeting in a school building on Sunday and in our home during the week. After a year of slow growth, I merged the church with a larger congregation, merging myself out of work.

After a couple years of part-time, temporary jobs, some friends suggested I try the post office because I would get high priority being a disabled vet. I did and became a mail handler at the St. Louis post office—this was an education! One evening in my first week, I was told to take large mail bags off a table and place them on their respective carts surrounding the table. The large bags, each with a name of a city, slid down a chute from the floor above to the table where I was working.

Things went well for thirty minutes or so, and then the bags came down in a flurry. Now I really began to work up a sweat. I was diving back and forth under the table, pushing full carts away and replacing them with empty carts. I began to think that I wasn't going to be able to handle this particular job. After an hour of very strenuous activity, another mail handler came by and said, "Hey, man, take it easy, there's supposed to be five people working this table." The boss was fortunate that I needed this job because I was ready to stuff him in a bag and send him to Dallas or someplace.

There were many good workers, and I had three good bosses in my twelve years in the post office. However, a large number of workers were interested only in paychecks, breaks, vacations, and in doing as little as possible. It appeared to me that all they were interested in was more benefits, less work, and no responsibility. While unloading trucks, the conveyer belt which carried the packages would sometimes go down, and a dozen or two mail handlers would be sitting on their hands for fifteen minutes to an hour at a time. Often, as soon as the line started again, they would take their twenty-minute break.

My cousin, who worked for a large union in Michigan, discovered, as I did, that if one tried to put in a good eight hours of labor for eight hours of pay, one would find himself in trouble with union thugs. The concept of working as onto the Lord or just doing a good job for the personal satisfaction of it is becoming a thing of the past. It appears to me that many people feel that the government and/or society owe them a comfortable life without any effort on their part.

After a short time as a mail handler, I became a letter carrier, which was much more to my liking; now I was outside and meeting many people. During my last four years in the post office, my route was under the flight pattern of the St. Louis International Airport. As I heard and saw the planes overhead, I often thought that I should be flying planes for four to five times the money I was making as dog bait. I berated myself for volunteering for Vietnam. I could have easily avoided the war and become a highly paid commercial pilot in 1967 with all my bones in their proper order and place. One thing that saved my sanity was thanking God for all I had. I had a great wife and family, two eyes, a hand at the end of each arm, a foot at the end of each leg, and I lived in freedom in America, the greatest country of all time. I had a job and a car in which to drive home. I find it is impossible to thank God for all I have and then complain at the same time.

After twelve years in the post office, I retired on a medical disability due to bad knees. The combination of marine training, a lot of basketball on concrete courts, and a few nasty falls while carrying mail on snow and ice, finished my knees. Five arthroscopic procedures followed by two knee replacements have taken me out of most of the sports that I enjoyed, but I can still hunt, fish, and play golf.

I also believe that God works everything for the best if we trust him. Even if we make mistakes, God uses everything to develop our character and bring us closer to him. I occasionally castigated myself for a decision I made after my second wound in Vietnam. At that time, I was offered a desk job which would have taken me out of the fighting for the rest of my tour. I would have returned home in late '66 and probably landed a good job with the airlines in early '68. Only God knows how I would have responded to all the amenities a large salary would have provided. I am sure that my relationship with my wife and family would have suffered had I had a lot of money for hunting, fishing, and golf excursions.

The bottom line is, that in spite of all that has happened since I decided to remain in my combat role, I have a great deal of contentment and satisfaction in knowing I did the right thing, even at great personal cost. To do well, whatever it is that God has called us and equipped us to do, and to trust him completely where ever that call takes us has its own great rewards. The world and its ways offer nothing of eternal value; only God provides comfort, peace, joy, and eternal blessings.

Ran Jansen

Diane Maloy

Ran-PrimaryFlt.Trng, T-34 aircraft, Fall-1962

T-28 Trainer carrier qualification
aboard the USS Lexington

H-34 helicopter intership transfer of supplies,
Summer 1964, Mediterranean Sea

H-34 somewhere in the Med. Sea area, Summer 1964

Home sweet home, pilots home in Vietnam, Spring 1966

Purple Heart award, May 1, 1966, ChuLai-Vietnam

Maloy-Jansen Wedding, July 16, 1966

Wedding, July 16, 1966

C-130 "Hercules" on the ramp at MCAS Cherry Point, NC

C-130 refueling A-4 attack jets-east of Bermuda

Canoe trip with brother, Canada
1971, 42 inch Northern Pike

Brother Ben—overcomes a large beaver dam, Canada 1971

Diane, Therea, and Craig Jansen, 1973

Ben, Alice Jansen, Craig, Diane, Ran and
Therea, 50th anniversary, 1991

Here I am inspecting the rotor head of my helo.
At this time I'm wearing a body armour vest.
When I got shot the last time I was not wearing it,
which probably saved me from more damage. The bullet
would have entered my arm at the opening in the vest
and then probably would have been turned back into my
upper back upon hitting the vest on the inside back.

TEN

In my early forties, I was out of work, and the peace and joy I had known most of my life was evaporating. The hostility and anger I had known in the early 70s had returned—by my allowing it to happen. Peace, joy, and calmness can not inhabit the same soul where there is hostility, anger, and resentment. Rethinking and reliving the Vietnam War and its aftermath was the catalyst for my dive into depression and ungodly attitudes. I was a fight looking for a place to happen.

Liberty and freedom cannot be obtained without the shedding of blood. Whether it is a war against tyranny, evil dictators around the world, or against crime and danger in our own cities and neighborhoods, someone is going to get hurt or killed. Military people, policemen, firemen, and first responders are on the frontline; I accepted this fact when I enlisted and again when I was commissioned. It is a fact that there is evil, pain, and suffering all over the world; I have seen it, and I have experienced it.

I believe my hostility and anger had its foundation in the way the war was handled by the politicians and reported by the media. Making a sacrifice is one thing, but to see that sacrifice misused, mishandled, or dismissed, is something else. I am aware of my disability every minute I'm awake, my chosen career was prematurely terminated, and many friends and acquaintances are injured or dead. I am fortunate, I live a normal life and continue in many activities, while many vets are blind, paralyzed, and suffer permanent mental disability. Millions of people in Laos, Cambodia, and Vietnam were maimed, killed; and many more had their lives and homes devastated. Instead of bringing peace and freedom, which could have been done, we condemned millions to savage dictatorships. In America's failure, we encouraged other evil people to continue to destroy peace and freedom around the world.

Questions roared through my head. Why is there war and evil? Why was the Vietnam War conducted in such an insane manor? Sometimes we were not allowed to return fire; bombing was started and stopped, and large areas were restricted to bombing. Our fighters could chase enemy planes to a certain point but were not allowed to destroy their airfields. Insignificant targets were hit repeatedly while critical targets were untouched. Ninety percent of the area from China to Hanoi was off limits to all bombing; this was the major trafficking corridor for missiles and weapons. Reconnaissance aircraft tracked surface to air missiles (SAMs) all the way from China to launch sites in North Vietnam, but we were not allowed to take them out until they became operational. The generals had little to say about the conduct of the war, while ignorant "whiz kids" ran the war from Washington.

Why did the media slant and misrepresent what was going on? Why did the media not tell the American people and the rest of the world about the campaign of terror waged by the communists? When a few US soldiers murdered about five hundred people at My Lai, the reporting was nonstop for months. At Phu Bai/Hue, four to six thousand Vietnamese civilians were murdered, but little or no reference was made in the media. Why? Because the communists did it! Why was it not reported?

The one-sided, anti-American reporting of the war led to a lack of support, which ultimately resulted in defeat for America as well as the people of Vietnam, Laos, and Cambodia. General Norman Schwarzkopf in his book, *It Doesn't Take a Hero*, tells of a directive from North Vietnam's leader, Ho Chi Minh, which was recovered in 1965 when a Vietcong headquarters was overrun. In effect Ho Chi Minh said this to his supporters: "I know you are facing more and more Americans right now, but don't worry. We're going to win the war against America the same way we won the war against the French; not on the battlefield, but in the enemy's homeland. All you have to do is hang on. The American people are not tough enough to see this war through, and we are. We have fought for twenty years; we can fight another twenty years; before then, they will give up and not support their troops anymore, and we will claim victory."

The American people were indoctrinated by the media with one-sided reporting, which led to the lack of support for the American effort and encouraged the enemy to continue the fight. A war that could have been won was not lost, but was thrown away. That leads to a huge question for those of us who are still paying the price: was it worth it? Are we just victims also, even though we fought with courage, honor, commitment, and self-sacrifice? Is there ever a reason to serve, self-sacrifice, or commit to anything that doesn't benefit us personally? If all is determined by meaningless, purposeless forces or survival of the fittest, then one should only show self-interest, self-preservation, and self-indulgence. Why would one bother to risk oneself for another's benefit?

Another question I asked: why is our society coming apart? When I was in high school, the major sins were making wise guy comments, chewing gum, skipping school, and throwing paper wads or paper airplanes (I never chewed gum in school). Now we need policemen in our schools because of theft, assault, rape, and murder.

Another major question I had since I was in high school: are science and the Bible compatible? Is it true that science is about reality, facts, and reason and is for intelligent, educated people, while the Bible is about belief, myth, and superstition for ignorant, poorly educated people who needed a "crutch" to get through life? Science says that macro-evolution is true and there is no God, but many intelligent scientists disagree and have concluded there must be a God. Who is right?

Why do many people fight the concept of intelligent design? Why do they avoid the concept of a supreme creator/designer? The fact is that science has been defined in a way which excludes even the possibility of there being a supernatural cause for all that exists. Why are we not allowed to go where the evidence leads?

There have been times of peace and joy throughout my life as you have read. However, the question is: was this just the result of believing myths and superstitions that had been handed down from parents, grandparents, church, and school? In other words, if I had sincerely believed that the Easter Bunny or a space alien was going to take me to the great fishing hole and golf course in the sky when I died, would that have given me peace and joy? Do we need to believe in something even if it isn't true?

All my life I had believed in a supreme being, a God who created the universe and everything in it. I believed he was a God of love, mercy, grace, and compassion who was interested in all we do and that he established standards by which we should live; and that He wanted to have a relationship with us through Jesus Christ.

Were my beliefs all wrong? Was this merely a false set of doctrines I had received growing up? Was this all nonsense? Is there truth, or is everything relative? Does everyone make up his own truth? Did the entire universe come about from nothing, without plan, without purpose, or without intelligence? If so, where did the concepts of freedom, liberty, love, and self-sacrifice come from? If all came about by accident, then these concepts are nonsense, completely irrational.

Of one thing I was certain: before I committed myself to anything where I could get hurt or cause myself any grief whatsoever, I was going to check out everything that I could. I wanted real answers.

The problem was that I didn't know where to begin. I wish now that I had kept a journal because I don't remember where I began; I started everywhere at once. I read books on philosophy, physics, astrophysics, logic, history, and religion. I read C. S. Lewis, R. C. Sproul, Philip E. Johnson, F. Schaefer, N. L. Geisler, and many others. I did a lot of thinking. I didn't even know the first question. The question concerning the existence of God is a good question, but it's not the first question or even the second question. Likewise, the question concerning the origin of the Bible is another good question, but again, it's not the first question. Finally, after a lot of studying, questioning, and thinking, I found the first question. It is very simple and yet profound.

ELEVEN

The first question is: is there anything? Some say nothing exists; everything we think we see is simply an illusion or a dream. I didn't spend much time considering the possibility that everything I see is nothing more than an illusion. The fact that those who believe everything is an illusion look both ways before crossing a street to avoid being whacked by an illusionary truck was enough for me. Were my wounds in Vietnam just a figment of my imagination? I think not! The answer to the first question is simply, "Yes, there is something." There is a massive, expanding universe with billions of galaxies, which are full of stars, black holes, novas, planets, meteors, asteroids, gas clouds, and other stuff. Our solar system is a sun around which planets revolve, including our earth, the third rock from the sun. On the earth, there are people, animals, birds, fish, trees, vegetation, air, rocks, water, sand, bugs, insects, bacteria, golf courses, and lots of stuff. Yes, there is something.

The second question is also simple: why is there something rather than nothing—why does anything exist? As far as I can tell, there are only three possibilities to explain why this incredible universe and everything in it exists.

The first possible explanation is that the universe has always existed—it is eternal, self-existing, and without a beginning. The second law of thermodynamics (entropy) destroys this argument. The universe is winding down. The amount of usable energy is decreasing; thus, if it had an infinite past, it would have run down by now. In fact, without a beginning, a starting point, we could not get to today. There must be a starting point, a beginning.

Some say the universe is like a bouncing ball, it comes to an end and bounces back; in other words the universe expands, runs out of energy, collapses in upon itself and then explodes into being again. A major problem here is that there's not enough mass in the universe to cause it to collapse; the universe is still expanding. Another set of questions: how did it start? How did it get wound up? Where did the mass come from in the first place? Who determined the power of the forces at work? The concept of an eternal, self-existing universe without beginning is irrational.

The second possible answer as to why there is something is that the universe is self-created. In effect, this idea says that nothing produced something and then this something produced everything. Basically this means that time and chance, plus material caused everything that exists. A couple of questions: "Where did the material come from? Who or what is chance?" Somehow time and chance are given a great deal of power. In reality, chance can do nothing; chance can merely give the odds of a coin coming up heads or tails.

No matter how much time is available, chance cannot produce or control anything—chance is nothing.

To think that nothing produced something, chaos produced order, non-life produced an infinite variety of intricately designed life forms, and that information, logic and intelligence came from nothing is absolutely illogical.

The concept of self-creation violates the law of causality. All of science is based upon the concept that there has to be an adequate cause behind every effect. The law of causality states that all finite, contingent things need to have an adequate cause to come into being—the universe and everything in it is finite and contingent. If there is an explosion, there has to be an explosive element and something to set it off. If one is sick, one goes to the doctor to find the cause. If one's car malfunctions, one goes to a mechanic. The fact is that most pioneers of science believed there was a God behind everything in the universe and that by investigation, examination, and study, we could determine how everything came to be and how it operates. The universe exhibits design, information, and intelligence, which indicates rationality. As rational human beings, we could determine how a rational God brought the universe and everything in it into existence. There is no way inanimate chemicals and materials can produce life, information and reason. If at one time there was no material, no energy, and no cause, how did anything get here? The law of non-contradiction also comes into play. It is impossible for something to exist and not exist at the same time; something cannot be true and false at the same time. The universe would have had to not exist and yet exist to produce itself—this is totally illogical. Unfortunately, this is the official creation story in American academia. Some say that there is a cause out there, but we haven't discovered it yet; however, it cannot be God.

The problem is that science has been defined to exclude everything except material and natural causes. No matter how much information is gathered and no matter where it points, it has become totally unacceptable to allow any concept of the supernatural. Science is supposed to go to the truth, wherever that may be, even if it means recognizing supernatural power and intelligence.

A major question is this: do reason and logic lead us to believe in a godless universe, or in a universe that is God-designed and God-governed? The honest, rational investigator should be willing to follow facts, logic, and reason to wherever the evidence will lead. All presupposition and prejudice should be set aside.

From looking at a lot of evidence and the writings of many people, it is apparent to me that the concept of a God-designed universe has been ruled out by those who refuse to go where the evidence leads; they hold fast to a material/natural explanation only. Furthermore, the proponents of a godless universe have declared that their position is the only one allowed in our national education system and government. The reason they do not want anyone who believes that there is a God to be allowed to speak is summed up by a comment attributed to Richard Dawkins: "It is absolutely safe to say that if you met somebody who claims not to believe in evolution, that person is ignorant, stupid, or insane (or wicked, but I'd rather not consider that)".

Basically, what Dawkins and other materialists/ naturalists say is that science is objective and religion is subjective (ie, science is knowledge, religion is belief; science is about facts, religion is about superstition). In short, natural evolution is science; a belief in a supernatural being behind the universe is nonsense religion. However, even Carl Sagan admitted that the concept of evolution was "only a theory." There is a growing number of scientists who are not religious but have rejected the whole concept of evolution.

Pierre P. Grasse, editor of the twenty-eight volumes of "Traite de Zoologie" and ex-president of the *Academie des Sciences* is considered to be the most distinguished of French zoologists stated: "The explanatory doctrines of biological evolution do not stand up to an in-depth criticism" (*The Evolution of Living Organisms).*

P. Lemonie, a president of the Geological Society of France and director of the Natural History Museum in Paris has concluded, "...the theory of evolution is impossible."

The book by Ramas and Ross, "Origins of Life", is an excellent work pointing out the impossibility that life and the information necessary to produce life came from nothing.

My favorite quote which is simple and comes to the point was made by David Berlinski, a premier mathematician; he says the concept of evolution is "nuts".

As knowledge increases, more evolutionists and atheists are beginning to recognize that there is indeed a God behind all creation. Anthony Flew, one of the world's most renowned atheists, shocked a group at a symposium in New York when he said that because he believed in following the evidence where ever it led, he now believed in the existence of God. The investigation into the DNA material was one of the things that led him to the reversal of his life long beliefs.

According to those who insist upon promoting evolution as the truth behind all life, it would be a violation of the so-called separation of church and state to even mention the idea that there might be a supernatural intelligence behind all that exist. Now that, I believe, is not only ridiculous but wicked.

Robert Jastrow, the founder and former director of NASA's Goddard Institute for Space Studies says there are three levels of evidence for a beginning: the motions of the galaxies, the laws of thermodynamics, and the life story of the stars. He also stated: "That there are what I or anyone would call supernatural forces that are at work is now, I think, a scientifically proven fact." Another time, Robert Jastrow said this, "Now we see how astronomical evidence leads to a biblical view of the origin of the world. The details differ, but the essential elements in the astronomical and biblical accounts of Genesis are the same: the chain of events leading to man commenced suddenly and sharply at a definite moment in time, in a flash of light and energy."

These are not comments one will ever hear in a public university or a school in the United States, nor will it appear in any chemistry, biology, or physics textbooks. It is obvious that the universe and all that is in it is real, not an illusion. It is also apparent that it had a beginning and could not possibly be self-created. This leaves only one option: there is a creator/designer, a transcendent being behind the creation who did not come to be in the universe. If anything exists, and the universe exists and had a beginning, then a self-existent, transcendent being becomes necessary. An uncaused being must necessarily exist. Aristotle called this being the first cause— the unmoved mover. A denial of the existence of God can only come about by the rejection of rationality. The concept of the universe coming into being by material/natural forces cannot stand up to reasonable inquiry.

Theologian Thomas F. Torrance, in describing the creation from nothing put it this way:

"The creation of the universe out of nothing does not mean the creation of the universe out of something that is nothing, but out of nothing at all. It is not created out of anything-it came into being through the absolute fiat of God's Word in such a way that whereas previously there was nothing, the whole universe came into being."

If there was anything that co-existed with God, then that material would be equal with God. Thus, it has to be that there would be nothing at all if God had not willed the universe into being.

I've never been in the top 20 percent of students in the schools I've attended, neither have I been in the top 20 percent of the crazies I've associated with over the years. However, it is apparent to me that there is a transcendent, eternal, powerful, all-knowing, intelligent, personal, creator, designer, God behind the universe and everything in it. To follow the world view of those who do not believe that there is a God behind everything is totally irrational. I believe in the world view that there is a God behind everything

TWELVE

It is apparent that there is only one reasonable, logical explanation for the existence of the massive, expanding, and absolutely fantastic universe we observe and study. The cosmological argument for the existence of a creator/designer says that there is a cosmos caused by something beyond itself; everything that has a beginning must have an adequate cause. Science now recognizes that the universe did have a beginning; the concept of an eternal, static universe has been rejected.

Another reason for believing in a supernatural creator/designer is the teleological argument; this argument simply says that if there is apparent design in anything there must be a designer. The universe and the life forms in it are incredibly complex. C. M. Stine (1882–1954), a former director of research for DuPont said: "The world about us, far more intricate than any watch, filled with checks and balances of a hundred varieties is marvelous even beyond the imagination of the most skilled scientific investigator, this beautiful and intricate creation, bears the signature of its Creator graven in its work."

Michael J. Behe, in his book *Darwin's Black Box,* describes the fantastically complex structure of the cell and other structures like the cilium and bacterial flagellum. There is no way these miniature machines could have come about by accident over a period of time without intelligence; all the parts had to be there all at once and assembled in the proper order. Like a mouse trap that can't function unless all the parts are put together correctly, these highly complex biological structures could not have evolved over time.

Another argument for the existence of a supernatural creator/designer is called the anthropic principle. Basically, the anthropic principle states that the universe and earth was designed for life, which indicates intelligence and a great deal of care.

Hugh Ross, in his book *The Creator and the Cosmos,* lists over thirty parameters which are essential for life on earth. For example, a tiny fraction of a percent change in the power of gravity would cause the stars to burn too hot or to not form at all. The moon has to be just the right size and distance from the earth, which has to be just the right size and distance from a star that has to be just the right size, composition, and age. The atmosphere has to have the correct amount of oxygen and inert gases.

Here are a few numbers to express how unlikely it is for the universe to come about by accident or chance: The number 10^6 is one million; 10^7 is ten million, the number 10^{14} is 100 trillion. The maximum number of planets in the universe is calculated to be 10^{22}. The possibility of 33 parameters coming together on one planet is 10^{42}. Believe it or not, it gets even more incredible, if the expansion rate of the universe changed one to the power of 10^{55} nothing would have existed at all.

The cosmological, teleological, and anthropic arguments indicate that this creator/designer has infinite power, infinite wisdom, knowledge, intelligence, and is self-existent and eternal. To believe that the universe and everything in it came about by accident or self-creation is irrational nonsense. Even a golf tee (a life-essential item) with no moving parts has a designer. To believe that a human cell, with the information that would take many books to contain, came about by accident is ridiculous. The odds of one protein molecule being formed by accident is one to 10^{60}, and a protein molecule is not as complex as a simple cell.

Another reason to believe in the existence of the infinite creator/designer is the moral argument. C. S. Lewis, R. C. Sproul, and others make a strong case for this concept. The question one must ask is this: what is the basis for establishing a moral standard? What determines whether something is right or wrong? Evolution or material/natural forces cannot explain the motive or intent for any action, morality merely becomes a description of "average" behavior.

Karl Marx, B. F. Skinner, and Francis Crick claim that all behavior is caused by economics, environment, or DNA. If this is true, then why or how can behavior change? Under this system, there is no sin or evil; whatever is, is simply the way it is. There is no moral standard.

The question then, if there is no moral standard, becomes "Sez who?" Who decides whether an act or thought is right or wrong? Are we to have an elite board of judges, scientists, social engineers, economists, medics, politicians, or psychologists to establish some sort of a moral standard? Who is to decide who will occupy these positions? The people with the most guns? 51 percent of the people? the people who can buy influence?

What will be the basis for this new system of moral standards? Pragmatism, whatever works? Survival of the fittest? Even the golden rule has no basis if everything is the result of impersonal, material, naturalistic forces.

These natural forces cannot produce reason, logic, or the concept of right or wrong. Moral values do exist; therefore, a supreme moral being must exist! This truth forces us to one of two possible alternatives: (1) morality is meaningless or (2) we are accountable to a supreme moral being. R. C. Sproul states it this way:

> Moral laws imply a Moral Law Giver.
> There is an objective moral law.
> Therefore there is a Moral Law Giver.

Moral laws prescribe what ought to be, not what is. We can not say that Hitler and the Nazis were wrong unless there is a standard above that which people and government say it is. The Nazis were not tried according to American law or German law, but by a standard set by a higher authority. If there is no God, we owe the Nazis—whom we executed—a huge apology.

Abraham Kuyper said, "All created life necessarily bears in itself a law for existence, instituted by God Himself." Kuyper went on to say that we must use these laws for human existence: we cannot be apart from these laws any more than we can separate ourselves from the physical laws.

Edmond Burke (1729–1797) said: "There is but one law for all, namely, the law which governs all law, the law of our Creator, the law of humanity, justice equity—the law of nature and nations."

In America and in the rest of the world, we have proof of the existence of the moral law established by God. Under God's system, there are moral requirements, which, if followed by governments and people, will lead to freedom and liberty. There are repercussions for those who fail to follow moral principles. Where there is no God, there is no standard of good and evil—whatever is, is. Therefore, we need more and more government to attempt to control the inevitable chaos which comes when everyone can decide for themselves what it right. Selfishness, self-indulgence, and lawlessness become the norm.

The final reason for believing in God to be discussed in this chapter is the principle of analogy, simply stated: being causes being. The being that caused all other beings cannot bring into other beings what the creating being does not have. The effect must be similar to the cause; we can see the designer in the design. By looking at the human being, we can see and appreciate traits/characteristics we could not possibly have received from evolution, a combination of chemicals and materials coming together by accident. We are creative, we have personality, we posses will/volition, we reason, plan, we can love, we establish relationships, we communicate, we can be happy, angry, we can forgive, we can give comfort, and we are willing to sacrifice ourselves for others and worthy causes. We appreciate honesty, integrity, loyalty, devotion, and we understand mercy and justice, for all these things, there is no materialistic/naturalistic explanation.

Another thing that caught my attention is this: if there was love, communication, and relationships before the universe was created, with whom was the Creator in relationship? Some say that God created the universe and people because he needed to have something and someone to relate to and love. I believe that God needed nothing—in fact, if God needs anything, he is not God. This indicates to me that there was and is more than one entity; each one is the same in eternal existence, holiness, completeness, and all the godly characteristics.

What has been discussed in this chapter is what one would call general revelation. By looking at the universe and everything in it, we can get a very clear picture of who God is, what he has done, and the fact that he has designed humans to have a relationship with him.

THIRTEEN

By now one of the major, most critical questions I raised in chapter 10 has been answered in the affirmative—there definitely is a God (creator/designer) of the universe, all of nature, and us humans. Through observation, reason, and logic, we have learned a great deal about him. This knowledge is apparent to anyone who examines all the evidence with an open and honest search for the truth.

The next question concerns another revelation about God. What about "religious" literature? When Hugh Ross, a brilliant scientist, came to the conclusion that there had to be a supreme being—a God—behind the universe he had thoroughly studied, he began a study to discover if any religious writings described everything the way it was.

In Ross's book *The Creator and the Cosmos*, he tells of his search through religious writings to see if there was anything that confirmed what he knew of history and science. He concluded that in all he examined "the sophistry and the incongruity with established facts seemed opposite to the Creator's character as suggested to me by nature." In other words, religious writings—except the Bible—are foolishness.

Concerning his study of the Bible, Ross had this to say, "Here was a journalist record of the earths initial conditions–correctly described from the standpoint of astrophysics and geophysics–followed by a summary of the sequence of changes through which earth came to be inhabited by living things and ultimately by humans. The account was simple, elegant, and scientifically accurate. From the stated viewpoint of an observer on earth's surface, both the order and the description of creation events perfectly matched the established record of nature. I was amazed."

Only the Bible offers a realistic explanation of the origins of the universe, all the creatures, and man. In addition, only the Bible offers the most comprehensive description of man and his condition. The Bible clearly tells us of the original condition of man, how man became such a mess, and the only way of permanently fixing the disaster.

God created humans in his image, in a perfect state, designed to have a relationship of love, honor, and communication with him. God did not want a robotic, puppet-like relationship, so he gave man free will, the power to make choices. Unfortunately, man did not want to be governed by God; he wanted to be God and thereby destroyed the relationship with God through defiance and disobedience. Man is now separated from God.

God has established the way to restore this broken relationship, but even here man wants to do it his own way rather than God's way. Man's "religions" try to fix that break by works, rules and regulations, rituals, meditation, or seeking "enlightenment" from aliens or other entities. Many do not want a relationship with God; they do not want any authority in their lives, so they become agnostic, atheistic, or develop their own religions with their own rules to serve gods of their own making and description. In this way, they can live their lives without constraint. They reject the idea of sin or evil in order to do whatever they desire without correction or consequences.

Because of man's separation from God, he is also separated from other men. The world is full of broken relationships, divisions, splits, arguments, and war. Man is basically self-centered, thinking only about his own pleasure, peace, and prosperity. Because of selfishness, marriages are falling apart, labor and management are at each other's throats, countries want what other countries have, and people are jealous of each other.

Man is also separated from himself. In spite of all the prosperity and good living in America, there is an ever growing amount of personal problems, hurts, and mental disorders. Man has turned to money, possessions, and status to become "fulfilled" and "complete"—but these things don't work and will never satisfy completely. A famous tennis player had it all—money, possessions, and women—yet he tried to kill himself because life was not fulfilling. A well-known writer stated that when he "got to the top" of success with money, possessions, and fame, there "was nothing there." Man was designed to have a relationship with his Creator. Without it, man is a forlorn, unfulfilled, disenchanted mess. Man then turns to drugs, alcohol, possessions, and monetary/ social success to find fulfillment.

Man is also separated from nature. Each year millions of people are killed by fleas, flies, mosquitoes, animals, snakes, tornados, hurricanes, floods, tidal waves, earthquakes, and drought. As bad as that is, here in America we've killed over 55 million babies because they are inconvenient. Thousands of other people are killed by drunk drivers, cigarettes, texting while driving, drugs, and criminals. Without God's salvation, his truth, and repentance; the problems of man will never be fixed. We have more and more chaos and trouble, yet man refuses to accept God's answers and turns instead to more government programs.

Only the Bible tells it the way it is; it corresponds to the reality we see all about us. Many say that God doesn't care. They say God "wound the world up" and then left it all to play itself out. It is inconceivable to me that the one who would bring about an elaborate, complicated, and intricate universe and all that is in it would simply "shrug his shoulders" and walk away. He, like us, wouldn't produce children, a house, a garden, art masterpieces, or anything else and then ignore it all. We teach, instruct, care for, and guide our children. He does the same. God left us the Bible, the manufacturer's handbook, to teach, instruct, guide, lead, and to give us standards by which we are to live and be productive.

Is the Bible God's Word, or just a collection of myths and legends? Following my search for truth, I believe that the evidence overwhelmingly supports the claim that the Bible is indeed God's special revelation to us. Norman Geisler and Peter Bocchino in their book *Unshakable Foundations* cover this subject very well. In chapter ten, Geisler and Bocchino state, "There is more abundant and accurate manuscript evidence for the New Testament than for any other book from the ancient world. Furthermore, there are more manuscripts copied with greater accuracy and earlier dating than for any secular classic from antiquity." They also reference many other scholars and sum it up with this: "...the New Testament is the most historically accurate and reliable document from all of antiquity."

Another reason for believing the Bible to be God's Word is the revelation of phenomena mentioned in the Bible long before these things became known by science. The Bible talks of the earth being round, the cycle of water, the circulation of air, the fact that life is in the blood, and the ocean currents. Admiral Matthew Fontaine Maury (1806–1873) was the first to chart the sea lanes and currents of the oceans. He was also the father of the US Naval Academy. One day, while he was sick, his son read Psalm 8 to him. Verse 8 mentioned the "paths" (or customary roads) of the sea. The mention of these paths inspired the admiral to investigate this phenomenon. As a result, he wrote the first book on the subject, and he became known as the father of oceanography. This information concerning the paths in the sea could only have come from the creator of the seas. When the Psalms were written well over 2,500 years ago, there was no one on earth who had knowledge of the paths.

Fulfilled prophecy is another indicator of the divine, supernatural source of biblical writings, no other religious writings contain prophecy that is later fulfilled. Detailed predictions, often written hundreds of years before the events, come true in exact historical fulfillment. In the case of Tyre, an important, well-defended seaport in the Mediterranean, prophecies were made telling of its coming destruction hundreds of years prior to the event....*I am against you, O Tyre— (many nations) will destroy the walls—I will scrape away her rubble and make her a bare rock—they will break down your walls and demolish your fine houses and throw your stones, timber and rubble into the sea—you will become a place to spread fishing nets. You will never be rebuilt—.* Ezekiel 26:3–14

Noman Geisler sums up the fulfillment of these prophecies in his book *Baker Encyclopedia of Christian Apologetics* with these words: "This prediction was partially fulfilled when Nebuchadnezzar destroyed the city and left it in ruins. However, the stones, dust and timber were not thrown into the sea. Then Alexander the Great attacked the seemingly impregnable Island of Tyre by taking the stones, dust, and timber from the ruined mainland city and building a causeway to the Island. Not only has the city never been rebuilt: today it literally is used as a place 'to spread fishing nets.'"

Prophecy concerning the crucifixion of Jesus was written long before this evil form of death was even invented. To have even a few prophecies concerning the life and death of an individual come true is virtually impossible. In the case of Jesus, there are more than three hundred prophecies, all fulfilled; the odds defy reason.

Archaeology also verifies the events and times of the Bible. W. F. Albright of Johns Hopkins University said, "There can be no doubt that archaeology has confirmed the substantial historicity of Old Testament tradition." Millar Burrows of Yale University has also stated that archaeology has added to the reliability of the Bible.

Keith N. Schoville in his book *Biblical Archaeology in Focus* says: "It is important to realize that archaeological excavations have produced ample evidence to prove unequivocally that the Bible is not a pious forgery. Thus far, no historical statement in the Bible has proven false on the basis of evidence retrieved through archaeological research."

The Bible and its story of Jesus could not have survived if the story of Jesus and his death and resurrection had been made up by his followers. After Jesus' death, his disciples were scared to death, hiding out, and had no intention of making up a story. After they met the risen Jesus, they were changed men—and most of them died rather than change their story. Many people are willing to die for a lie—but not if they know it is a lie.

The fact that women were mentioned in the story indicates they were telling the truth. In that day, women had no credibility, so no one would use women in fabricating a lie. The disciples simply told it the way it was without fabrication, without consideration of the possible consequences of what anyone would think or believe; they merely stated the facts. Hundreds of people met Jesus and verified his resurrection within forty days. This is not a legend; legends take several generations to develop.

The Bible is not the only source of information concerning the life and crucifixion of Jesus Christ. Secular historians of the first and second centuries also refer to Jesus and his followers. Thallus (AD 52) and Phlegon (AD 80–140) refer to Jesus and also mentioned the earthquake and darkness at the time Jesus was crucified. Pliny the Younger (AD 61–113) tells of Jesus's followers singing hymns to Jesus who they believed is God. He also said the Christians made oaths to be morally pure in all areas of their lives.

Suetonius (AD 69–140) wrote of the Christians believing Jesus to be God and thereby being able to die courageously for their commitment to Jesus. Tacitus (AD 56–120) accounted for the fact that Jesus lived in Judea, was crucified under Pontius Pilate and that the followers of Jesus were severely persecuted. Mare Bar-Serapion (AD 70) testified to the fact that Jesus was a real person with great influence and referred to Jesus as the Wise King.

Lucian of Sarasota (AD 115–200) and Celsus (AD 175) wrote about Jesus and Christians in a very sarcastic way but verify that these were real people and that the miracles of Jesus were believed. Josephus (AD 37–101), the Jewish historian, described the death of John the Baptist, the execution of James, the brother of Jesus, and said that Jesus was a wise man.

Lee Strobel covers the resurrection very well in his book *The Case for Easter*. Lee's other books *The Case for*

Christ, The Case for A Creator, and *The Case for Faith* should be read by every believer who wants to be able to give a reason for their faith.

Here's an interesting question: what would it take for you to believe your brother is God and has been raised from the dead? Well, James, the half-brother of Jesus, believed and paid for it with his life. Before the resurrection, the brothers of Jesus did not believe that Jesus was God. They met Him after the resurrection and were convinced that Jesus was the Messiah.

The tomb of Jesus had been guarded by the toughest soldiers of the time, and they would have been executed for allowing the body to be stolen. Even the enemies of Jesus testified to the fact of the empty tomb.

The early church that followed Jesus would never have survived if it hadn't been for the overwhelming evidence that Jesus did indeed rise from the dead. They gave their lives for the fact of the resurrection. Also, the fact that these early believers were almost all Jews and that they changed their day of worship to Sunday indicates a firm belief in the resurrection.

Sir Lionel Luckhoo is in the record books as being one of the world's most successful attorneys. After analyzing the resurrection for several years, he said this: "I say unequivocally that the evidence for the resurrection of Jesus Christ is so overwhelming that it compels acceptance by proof which leaves absolutely no room for doubt."

Another famous lawyer who wrote the standard work on legal evidence, Dr. Simon Greenleaf, a law professor at Harvard Law School said this: "Having for many years made the evidence of Christianity the subject of my close study, the result has been a firm and increasing conviction of the authenticity and plenary inspiration of the Bible, it is indeed the Word of God."

Many people have said that Jesus was a great man and moral leader, but he was not God. C. S. Lewis (1898–1963) was an atheist until he investigated the claims of the Bible. He had this to say about that idea: "A man who was merely a man and said the sort of things that Jesus said would not be a great moral teacher, he would either be a lunatic—on a level with the man who says he is a poached egg—or else he would be the devil of hell. You must make your choice. Either this man was, and is, the Son of God, or else a madman or something worse."

Jesus said he is God. This is either true or false; there are no other options. If it is false, there are only two options: 1) He knew he wasn't God but said he was—that makes him a liar. 2) He thought he was God but was not—that makes him a lunatic. A liar or lunatic cannot be a great man and a moral leader; a man like this should be disregarded completely. Jesus is God, eternally. He added humanity to himself in order to show us God and to pay for our sin.

I believe the evidence establishes without a doubt that the Bible is God's word. Just as a human father wishes to communicate with and instruct his children for the best life possible, so God has reached out to us to establish a relationship with himself through Jesus.

FOURTEEN

One of the questions I expressed in chapter 10 I have yet to discuss; that is the question concerning the compatibility of science and the Bible. I believe the evidence proves that God created the universe and everything in it. I also believe the evidence proves God is the ultimate source of the Bible. It is obvious that the forty writers of the Bible represent different levels of learning, different personalities, and some differences in culture, considering the Bible was written over a period of about 1,400 years. However, God influenced ("breathed into") the writers in a way that God's chosen words were expressed through the personalities of the writers.

God is true in word and action; therefore, what he has created cannot be in conflict with what he has said. Accurate, factual science and the correct interpretation of the Bible of necessity must be in 100 percent agreement.

Science has verified many things in the Bible; and therefore, science is not a threat to the Bible. The theory of macroevolution is not science and cannot stand up to honest investigation. Even if there were billions of times more years than the 13.7 billion years from the beginning of the universe until now, evolution is impossible. No amount of time can make nothing into something or non-life into the countless forms of life we now see—it is scientifically impossible. Information cannot come from inanimate chemicals and material; there must be intelligent planning behind all we see. There are scientists who admit that evolutionists have a commitment to ignore anything that indicates a supernatural cause behind the universe. The theory (it has never gone past being a theory) of evolution is being destroyed as real scientific knowledge progresses. To continue to believe in evolution as the answer behind all creation is irrational nonsense. Unfortunately, many Christians came to believe that in order to fight the theory of evolution, they had to limit the time of the creation process. As a result, they hold fast to the concept of six literal twenty-four-hour days in which creation took place six to ten thousand years ago.

God is true, honest, intelligent, unchanging, and the source of all learning, reason, and logic. His laws are immutable and permanent. God is not in the business of making things to appear different from what they are. Most of the early scientists believed we humans are rational beings created by a supreme, rational being; therefore, humans should be able to discover how the Creator brought everything into being and the processes behind it. It is no accident that our location in a specific part of the right type of galaxy, in the optimal place in the universe gives us a prime location to observe the rest of the universe.

Through science, we can now see and know how stars are formed. We see stars in many different stages of development from those just beginning to burn to those that have expired and blown up. In 1987, a supernova (an old sun burns out, collapses in on itself, and blows up) was seen by astronomers. This supernova (SN1987A) blew up in another galaxy 170,000 years ago. If, as some say, God made the stars look like they are different ages when in fact they were all created 6,000 to 10,000 years ago, it makes me wonder, what else is God fooling us about? Was Jesus really raised from the dead—or did God make it look like a resurrection by substituting a look-alike?

It is apparent that there was an initial explosion approximately 13.7 billion years ago. The question that needs to be asked is this: who was behind the big bang and who put all the finely tuned laws of physics into place? The tiniest change in the force of gravity (1 to the power of 10^{37}) or in the rate of acceleration (1 to the power of 10^{55}) would preclude the possibility of development of any kind. It is a fact that the galaxies furthest away from us are moving away at a faster rate than those closer to us. This is a clear indication that the entire universe came from a single point.

The life cycle of the stars, the expanding universe, and the unchanging laws of God indicate that the universe had a beginning a long, long time ago by our measurement of time. To say that the six days of creation were six twenty-four-hour days that began 6,000 years ago flies in the face of logic, reason, accurate scientific mesurement, and scripture itself.

The Hebrew word for day is *yom*, and is used as we use the word *day* today; it can mean a twenty-four-hour period, it can be day as opposed to night, or it can be used to describe an age as we might say "the day of the horse and buggy." Some have tried to make the case that when *yom* is used with a number (ie, day 1, day 2, etc.) that this refers to a twenty-four-hour period—this is not correct; context gives the true interpretation. Early Hebrew writers never used the phrase "from evening to morning" to refer to a twenty-four-hour day; they would use the phrase "from morning to morning" or "from evening to evening." The Hebrew language at that time did not have a word for eon or anything else to refer to a long period of time.

It is also interesting to note that the root word for evening is *chaos* and the root word for morning is *order*, thus each period of creation was taken by God from chaos to order.

Another point is this: if the seven days were describing seven twenty-four-hour periods, why is there no evening and morning for day seven? I believe we are in the seventh day in that we are in the period of time after the creation of the universe.

Let's look at what took place on the sixth day: God made the animals, God formed man, planted the garden, and Adam named thousands of animals (probably after observing their behavior in order to come up with an appropriate name, although the Bible doesn't say that explicitly). Also on the sixth day, Adam searched for a mate. The Bible states that no suitable helper was found for him. Adam falls asleep, and Eve is made from his rib and is then presented to Adam. The interpretation of that passage indicates that Adam's helper is finally, at long last presented to him. This does not sound like a twenty-four-hour day to me.

Bishop Ussher determined that Adam was created about 4004 BC based on the assumption that the Hebrew word for *son* meant immediate son. In reality, the word *son* can mean *offspring* or *descendant*. Norman Geisler, in his book *Baker Encyclopedia of Christian Apologetics*, states that the genealogies are open; there are many gaps in the lists of a person's descendants. Geisler states in one area of the discussion that it is implausible that Nahor died before his great, great, great, great, great, great grandfather, Noah. Another problem indicated in Geisler's book is that Moses must have been born more than 350 years after Kohath, his "grandfather," a time when the life span had been reduced to 120 years.

In reality it makes no difference to me in my Christian life whether Adam and Eve were created 6,000 years ago or 60,000 years ago. Neither does it matter in my life whether God developed the universe beginning with a big bang 13.7 billions years ago, or whether he popped it into existence a shorter time ago. What means everything to me though is that God made it. He knows my coming and going, and he loves me.

God is true. I see no conflict between accurate science and the correct interpretation of the Bible. As Christians, we need to attack the theory of evolution on the basis of science, not on the belief of a 6,000- to 10,000-year history. The theory of evolution dismisses God; the result is increasing chaos in our world. Philip

E. Johnson is correct in stating that Christians need to begin with the epistle of John, chapter 1, verse 1: "In the beginning there was Logos." *Logos* indicates reason, intelligence, logic, and information. God is the source of the beginning. There cannot be intricate design without information and infinite intelligence behind it. The universe and everything in it as well as the Bible have the same source — GOD.

The evidence is plain, obvious and overwhelming: there is a creator/designer God behind the universe and everything in it; and the Bible is his manufacture's handbook to the human race which he created in his own image. As far as I can tell, there are no other logical, reasonable answers to the questions I raised in chapter ten. God is truth and he is the reason behind our capacity to understand the concepts of moral standards, freedom, liberty, honor, justice, mercy, self-sacrifice and every good thing.

For those who want to further investigate the questions and issues raised, the bibliography will provide a tremendous volume of information. In fact, the bibliographies contained in the works of my bibliography could keep one reading and studying for many years.

I do recommend one book, "I Don't Have Enough Faith To Be An Atheist," by Norman Geisler and Frank Turek. This book should be read by every Christian and anyone who is sincere in their desire to know the truth.

This has been the story of my journey in search of the truth. The rest of the book concerns the issues of how we should live and the consequences of not living according to God and his word.

FIFTEEN

Why in the face of an incredible and overwhelming amount of evidence would one not believe in God as the creator/designer of the universe and the author of the Bible? Why are many people reluctant to discuss, investigate, or examine the evidence?

I believe there is one major reason many do not want to believe in God. However, the reason is not mentioned; only excuses come forth. These excuses may have real emotion, feelings, and experiences behind them, but these excuses do not hold up to logical, reasonable, examinations of the facts.

The prime reason people don't believe in God is that they don't want to believe—they don't want there to be a God because they inherently know that if there is a God, they are responsible to him. The unbeliever wants only to do his own thing without restraint or consequences, answering only to himself and his self-made standards.

Merv Griffin once asked the late Julian Huxley, a leader among Darwinists, why people believed in evolution. Huxley answered, "The reason we accepted Darwinism even without proof, is because we didn't want God to interfere with our sexual mores."

Lee Strobel, an atheist who became a Christian after looking at the evidence, said this: "I was more than happy to latch onto Darwinism as an excuse to jettison the idea of God so I could unabashedly pursue my own agenda in life without moral constraints."

Most people do things they know are wrong. Even if one doesn't believe in God, they know some things shouldn't be done. Sex is up front in the area of bad behavior. God designed sex in the framework of marriage between a man and a woman, but our society has gone in an entirely different direction of fostering homosexuality, pornography, and sex outside of marriage. Those involved in this do not want to change.

Many others are involved in other sorts of ungodly behavior such as fraud, stealing, lies, distortions, scams—all things they inherently know are wrong, but again, they do not want to change. It is easier to dismiss God than to change one's behavior. Poverty does not cause crime; lack of strong moral standards cause crime. Crime and fraud come from many well-educated, wealthy people—consider for example ENRON, Bernie Madoff, Wall Street scams, and organized crime.

Rev. Robert Hall in his book *Modern Infidelity Considered* (1836) says, "Infidelity is the joint offspring of an irreligious temper and unholy speculation, employed, not in examining the evidence of Christianity, but in detecting the vices and imperfections of confession Christians."

From a logical and reasonable examination of scientific and other evidence, it is obvious that the

Creator exists and has established moral standards. Atheists and evolutionist cannot possibly win the discussion with logic and facts, so they resort to ad hominen attacks. They attack the Christians personally.

Closely associated with the sense of lawlessness is the concept of self-fulfillment and self-centeredness. If there is no God, one can be free to act only in self-interest without regard for others. When one is totally committed to self, there is no looking out for the feelings or welfare of others. One of the dangers in becoming prosperous and successful is that one can wallow in self-indulgence, collecting possessions and self-promotion. If there is a God, one knows there are standards by which one must abide. Dismiss God and one can do what one wants—this, I believe, is the major reason people dismiss God even though there is a God-awareness built into everyone.

There are several excuses people use to dismiss or avoid God. One of the common excuses is that many have at sometime in their life been hurt, embarrassed, or in some way have been taken advantage of by a pastor, priest, teacher, or someone recognized as an authority figure within the "church." If one has been seriously hurt, it is easy to see why they want nothing to do with what they think is connected with God.

Although I've never had a really bad experience with church people, I've had a few unhappy dealings with some within the church and have met others that I would not want around my chicken house after dark. I'm sure there are those who would not want me in their neighborhood either. However, no matter what church people have done—witch hunts, crusades, false preacher/evangelists who steal money, church members who rip off others on Monday—none of these things destroy the evidence for a loving, caring, providing God who works for man's benefit on this earth and wants to have a relationship with everyone.

Observing professing Christians who behave poorly is not a legitimate reason to ignore God. Many people have been destroyed by drugs—yet I'm sure that if one is sick, one will take drugs prescribed by one's doctor. Others have been destroyed by a sudden influx of a large amount of money—yet I'll bet you wouldn't turn down a couple of million dollars if I offered it to you. God is for you—don't let a bad experience with someone from the church keep you from a personal relationship with the Creator of the universe, who loves you more than anyone else in the world.

Another reason many don't want to accept God is that they simply do not want to change their minds about anything. If one changes his opinion about anything, one knows that it will result in changed or destroyed relationships. People are generally locked into a certain belief system inherited from their parents, friends, and society. They prefer to stay in their comfort zone; to change one's ideas is to buck the family, the group, or others in their profession. Change can hurt. Even in the church, I've seen people hurt by their family and friends if they make a move into a different denomination. Leaving the family religion can mean being an outcast or being disenfranchised. In some societies, it can lead to death.

Another major excuse/reason for dismissing God concerns the problem of suffering and evil in the world. Why is there suffering? This is a valid question. The questioning goes like this: if God is good and all powerful, why is there trouble and evil? If evil exists, doesn't that mean God doesn't have the power to stop it? If God could stop it, but doesn't, then he isn't good. Why follow someone who isn't all powerful or good?

My initial response to those questions is this: how does one know that evil or good exists? If there is no God, what standard is there to determine if something is good or evil? Whatever the situations or conditions are—that is simply the way it is. There is no standard to judge whether it is good or bad, right or wrong. However, I definitely believe there is evil and suffering in the world. I've seen plenty and have experienced it—it is unavoidable.

If God wanted to avoid evil, he could have not created the universe, or he could have made us all puppets without the concept of free will. However, without free will, we are nothing. God created us in his image—we can choose, we can decide, we have creativity, we are something, we are valuable. Without free will, we are puppets. Unfortunately, each of us wants to do our own will and rebel against God. Like the devil and Adam and Eve, we don't want to worship God; we want to be sovereign in ourselves, so we go our own way.

The dysfunctional marriages, the divorces, the unwanted children, the pain, suffering, and cost to society are uncountable. Whose fault is that? God told us how to live, but sometimes we go another way. Lying, cheating, stealing, drug and alcohol abuse, voting for scoundrels, and refusing to help people fight tyranny—most of the sufferings in the world are man-made.

God can and will stop this madness one day. In the meantime, our problems are designed to bring us to him and for us to show his love to those in need. If we were never sick, never had any problems, and if we had everything in the world we wanted to satisfy every desire, why look to God?

In his wisdom, God allowed us to be free, and he has the power to work out all the problems for good. Without pain and suffering, with only success and pleasure, we would be totally hedonistic and never seek him. Without trials and tribulation on this earth, God's love and compassion simply could not be demonstrated through his people to those who are hurting and in need.

There is no simple, clear answer to the perplexing questions of pain and suffering; but the existence of pain and suffering does not prove that God does not exist or that he doesn't care. The suffering of those who suffer for reasons other than their own misconduct are the most difficult to understand. The baby born to a drug addict, children living in countries controlled by a vicious dictator—these are opportunities for good people to do good.

Most problems we face, however, are due to our own misconduct. For example, if I tell my son that if he will make his bed, do his chores, and not give his parents back talk, I'll take him fishing Saturday morning. If he fails to do right and disobeys instructions or disrespects his mother, he is not going fishing. Now whose fault is that? Certainly not the fathers. God set the rules, we decide to obey or not.

We overeat, eat wrong things, do not exercise, hold grudges, lose our temper, are unforgiving, hostile—all this will lead to problems. I've talked to many doctors over the years, and I've been told that the majority of our physical problems come from misbehaving. The percentage of physical maladies caused by poor lifestyles and bad attitude is between 50 to 90 percent, depending on which doctor one talks to.

Obviously, a baby has no control over his genes or the actions of his parents. If that baby suffers from congenital problems or bad behavior, it is not his/her fault, but it does show we all have responsibility to operate in this life according to God's standards and to be his hands and feet upon this earth. We are here to show God's love and provision to the hurting world. God often allows suffering in order to get our attention and draw us to him during difficult times. How can we be so bold as to question God? We don't have all knowledge and wisdom—we cannot see the whole picture, God is far above and beyond us in our meager insight. As kids, we didn't know even a fraction of what our parents knew and experienced; they could provide for and guide us because they knew a lot more than we did. God is a million times more above us than our parents. Who are we to question God? There are no logical, reasonable excuses to deny God or his provision for us. The evidence is that he's there; he loves us and wants a relationship with us.

Here are the two options as I see it: one can follow God and live according to his standards, or one can reject God and do his own thing. Following God's standards will lead to order, freedom, peace, joy and wholeness which is permanent and has at the end of our lives on earth glorious heaven for all eternity.

Doing ones own thing leads to chaos, disorder, fear, anxiety, grief and hell for all eternity. Why would one choose his own way over God's way?

SIXTEEN

One of the questions I raised in chapter ten concerns the decay of the American society. We see more mental illness, suicide, divorce, drug and alcohol addiction, abortion, fraud, lack of commitment to ones job and a general sense of unhappiness and discontent. We also see more people who believe their problems are not their fault, and therefore society and government are responsible to take care of them.

In corporations and government we see misconduct, fraud, misappropriation of funds, deceit, lying and a general lack of responsibility or care for their employees or constituents. Government is also starting to infringe on our rights and freedoms.

What is the source of the decay? One has to look no further than the official creation story promulgated by the evolutionists, the media and national education system. Basically this creation story says that by natural, random processes of genetics and natural selection man came about without plan or purpose.

Under this system of thought (worldview), which is the only accepted explanation of life admitted into the nation's secular (government) schools, it becomes clear why we are going down. Man decides what is right and wrong without regard to any supreme moral being. The insane part of this is that if all is without purpose, then any discussion of morality is meaningless. Morality becomes what one prefers, not what one ought to do, and this changes with time, there is no standard. A US senator, in the course of examining a Supreme Court nominee, stated that standards change as man decides; man becomes the ultimate authority.

So now we are at a point of changing to flexible standards of morality. As I questioned in chapter twelve, who decides? To once again quote Edmund Burke (1729–1797): "There is but one law for all, namely, that law which governs all law, the law of our Creator, the law of humanity, justice, equality—the law of nature and nations."

Thus we have two world views. One says that there is no standard of conduct, no law which holds everyone accountable. The other says that we are responsible to the supreme creator of all. These two worldviews are totally opposite; there is no room for compromise, following one or the other can only lead to conflicting actions and policies. We are either the product of a Creator who has set standards for us, or we are nothing. Ideas have consequences, whatever worldview one holds dictates how one will live and determine one's destiny.

The poet Samuel Smiles put it this way:

> Sow a thought, reap an act.
> Sow an act, reap a habit.
> Sow a habit, reap a character.
> Sow a character, reap a destiny.

The US was established on Judeo-Christian principles based upon the Bible—a fact that has been thrown out of American high schools, colleges, and universities. Quotes from the founding fathers have a biblical base, 94% of the quotes directly or indirectly refer to the Bible. William J. Federer has put together an extensive list of quotations from the Founding Fathers, presidents, and many other sources in *America's God and Country Encyclopedia of Quotations.* Henry Wilson (1812–1857), who was a US senator and vice president to President Grant, said:

"Men who see not God in our history have surely lost sight of the fact that, from the landing of the Mayflower to this hour, the great men whose names are indissolubly associated with the colonization; Rise and progress of the Republic have born testimony to the vital truths of Christianity."

Speaking of the *Mayflower*, here are a couple of the pertinent lines in the *Mayflower* compact. They begin with: "In the name of God, Amen." The second paragraph begins like this: "Having undertaken, for the glorie of God, and advancements of the Christian faith and honour of our King & countrie, due by these presents solemnly & mutually in the presence of God, and one another, covenant & combine our selves into a civill body politick…" (Spelling is as it appeared in the original) It is clear from what these people wrote and agreed to that God was the center of their lives, and they lived it. They were committed to God and each other.

Here is the current reference to the *Mayflower* compact as printed in the *Family Encyclopedia of*

Americas History and most American history text books: "...to form a 'Civil Body Politick' for our better Ordering and Preservation...To enact constitate and frame...just and equal Lawes...As shall be thought most meete and convenient..."

This is a clear attempt to rewrite American history by completely removing references to God and his design for American law and morality. Our early fathers were influenced by John Locke (1632–1704), the English philosopher who said: "He (Jesus Christ) was sent by God, His miracles show it: and the authority of God and His precepts cannot be questioned. His morality has a sure standard that revelation voucher, and reason cannot garner or question; but both together witness to come from God, the great Lawgiver."

George Washington made very plain his views on the source of all legitimate authority in his inauguration on April 30, 1789, when he said: "It would be peculiarly improper to omit, in this official act, my fervent supplication to that Almighty Being, who rules over the universe, who presides in the council of nations, and whose providential aid can supply every human defect, that His benediction may consecrate to the liberties and happiness of the people of the United States... Every step by which they have advanced seems to have been distinguished by some providential agency. We ought to be no less persuaded that the propitious smiles of Heaven can never be expected on a nation that disregards the eternal rules of order and light, which Heaven itself has ordained."

James Madison, in 1778, while addressing the general assembly of the state of Virginia stated, "We have staked the whole future of American civilization, not upon the power of government, far from it. We've staked the future of all our political institutions upon our capacity…to sustain ourselves according to the Ten Commandments of God."

There is no question the vast majority of the signers of the Declaration of Independence and the Constitution were men who believed that there could be no real peace, liberty, or freedom in a society without the governing of God based upon the Bible. At least twenty-nine of the signers had degrees from seminaries, yet today our students are being told these men were deists or atheists.

Throughout our history, many leaders have talked of the absolute importance of maintaining a focus on God and his ways in conducting our lives and government. No one has said it better than President Lincoln in his National Fast Day proclamation: "We have grown in numbers, wealth and power as no other nation has ever grown. But we have forgotten God…and we have vainly imagined, in the deceitfulness of our hearts, that all these blessings were produced by some superior wisdom and virtue of our own. Intoxicated with unbroken success, we have become too self-sufficient to feel the necessity of redeeming and preserving grace, too proud to pray to the God that made us! It behooves us, then to humble ourselves…to confess our national sins, and to pray for clemency and forgiveness."

Calvin Coolidge (1872–1933), the thirteenth president, said: "The foundations of our society and our government rest so much on the teaching of the Bible that it would be difficult to support them if faith in these teachings would cease to be practically universal in our country."

Thomas Jefferson said: "The Christian religion…is a religion of all others most friendly to liberty, science, and the freest expression of the human mind."

In 1947, Peter Marshall, the chaplain of the US Senate said this: "The choice before us is plain: Christ or chaos, conviction or compromise, discipline or disintegration. I am rather tired of hearing about our rights and privileges as American citizens. The time is come–it is now–when we ought to hear about the duties and responsibilities of our citizenship. America's future depends upon her accepting and demonstrating God's government."

Ronald Reagan put a more modern connection to all that has been said by countless fathers and contributors to the greatest country that ever existed when he said this: "If we ever forget that we are One Nation, Under God, then we will be a Nation gone under."

The founding of America was on Christian principles, and the founders knew that if we ever got away from that, it would all be over. Now we have thrown out God and his Word; the result is increasing chaos and dysfunction in the lives of individuals, families, and society overall. There is no sense of individual responsibility or moral standards. There are two forms of control for human actions: (1) restraint of conscience and (2) restraint of weapons or some sort of tyranny. The less we have of the first, the more we will have of the second.

The American form of government (the most successful in human history) was based on the concept of there being a Creator/God who has established standards of behavior for the government and the governed—our entire system is based on moral responsibility and civic duty, only Christianity gives the proper balance of form and freedom. When Christian principles are gone, chaos comes in; to stop chaos requires more tyranny imposed by the government.

Unfortunately, the far left who have no God (except themselves) and no absolutes (except "do whatever you want") now control the media, entertainment industry, the education system, and are close to being in control of the judicial system. The left goes crazy when we speak of God in absolutes. They have only one virtue—tolerance—which means they want everyone (except Christians) to be free to do/think whatever they want without restraint or conviction.

Now I began to understand the slanted reporting of the Vietnam War, reporting that still continues today. In the liberal mind, it makes no difference whether one chooses the American system or communism; one is not more right than the other—both are "true," so we shouldn't impose our system on another country. If the communists want to control the populace by the tyranny of murder and violence, who are we to say that it is wrong? The media believed that we were wrong to try to free South Vietnam, so they told lies and half-truths, and failed to mention the atrocities of the communists; but they were delighted to report US misconduct.

In the liberal mind, the woman who feeds her ten-day-old baby to the crocodiles in the river is just as right as the woman who takes her ten-day-old baby to church for a christening ceremony. The left is violently opposed to God and his kingdom. Their goal is to marginalize Christians whenever and wherever they can, and the media feeds this concept.

Activist judges make laws without regard to the Constitution, which many—including a Supreme Court justice and some high level US officials—want to get rid of the Constitution and take the laws from the UN or other countries.

If there is no purpose or meaning behind our being here, why bother with anything? Let everything fall apart and rot, what difference does it make? Why try to improve the lives of the poor, sick, or disabled? Just kill them. This was the Nazi policy—to get rid of the undesirables, the unfit, anyone who put a strain on society.

Obviously, the naturalists/materialists cannot live up to the logical outcome of their basic belief system, which is to let it all go, so they worship mother earth and demand that everyone live up to their standard, which is tolerance for everything except that which they don't like: the Christian worldview.

Our county has only one problem: we threw God and his Word out. All the problems we face are really symptoms. Only by restoring God and his Word in ourselves, our families, and our government can the root problem be fixed. Government programs will not fix anything; they don't take God's Word into consideration. William Penn said, "Those who will not be governed by God will be ruled by tyrants."

Not only did the Founding Fathers and many other Americans believe that God is the reason behind America's success. Charles Habib Malik (1906–1967) was ambassador to the UN from Lebanon and a member of the UN Security Council and made the following statement in 1958: "The good in the United States would never have come into being without the blessing and power of Jesus Christ...Whoever tries to conceive the American word without taking full account of the suffering and love and salvation of Christ is only dreamingThe irrefutable truth is that the soul of America is at its best and highest, Christian."

As we remove God and the precepts of Christianity from our individual lives, from our families, our society and government, chaos and trouble will increase. God will allow the natural consequences of our behavior to take over. Because of the increasing misconduct, irresponsibility and disregard for God's standard of morality, there will be more chaos which will cause the government to become more tyrannical.

How did we get to this point of decay? The next chapter will look at the Old Testament and the history of Israel. Israel often suffered because it ignored God and took the idols and customs of it's wicked neighbors as it's own. In A.D.70 Israel was destroyed because it failed to repent, declaring Caesar as it's god.

SEVENTEEN

When I was a youngster in Holland, Michigan, I learned a phrase concerning the relationship between the Old and New Testaments which goes: "The New is in the Old contained, the Old is by the New explained." The Old Testament is filled with forms, examples, and types (forerunners) that come alive in spiritual reality in the New Testament. For example, Moses led the people out of slavery in Egypt and Jesus leads the people out of the slavery of sin, Moses is a "type" of Jesus Christ.

Another example is Joshua, who leads the people out of the wilderness into the promised land. Jesus takes the people from the wilderness of sin into the promised land of God's kingdom. Not only is the action similar, Joshua and Jesus are the same names—Joshua is Hebrew and Jesus is Greek. Joshua, like Moses, is also a "type" of Jesus Christ.

The Old Testament temple was also a "type" of Christ. The temple is where the priests of the people came to meet with God and to offer the sacrificial blood of animals; again a "type" of Christ. In John 2:19, Jesus makes it clear that the old temple will be replaced because he will be the way to God, not a building or animal blood.

Israel in slavery, in Egypt, represents all people of all time. We are all sinners in bondage to sin just as Israel was in bondage to the Egyptians. When in Egypt, the Israelites had no army, no weapons, no leadership, no allies; they had no resources to set them free (if they had had a few marines, they might have had a good chance). As sinners, we too are without hope of being free. We have no resources of our own; there are no religious rules or rituals that can pay the price for our sin. We have no merit nor can we earn any merit through religion or anything else.

Because God is just, he cannot simply overlook our sin, just as our judges cannot simply set someone free because they feel sorry for the guilty person. There must be punishment for misbehavior; whether it is a three-year-old who violates home rules or a murderer, there absolutely and positively must be punishment. Unfortunately, the secular progressives/liberals hate this. They believe no one is responsible for anything they do. Christians and hardworking people, of course, are responsible for bailing out or otherwise taking care of those without a sense of responsibility.

There must be payment for crimes or misbehavior. The sacrificial blood of animals was inadequate, but there must be a blood sacrifice to pay for sin. The only one who can satisfy the death penalty we all are under is a perfect, sinless human—but there aren't any. Only God himself can pay the price; this is why the eternal triune person of the Trinity, the Son, added humanity to his person and paid the price no one could pay.

Just as God supernaturally took Israel out of slavery, God takes those who accept his sacrifice out of the bondage of sin and into his kingdom. There is no way to enter God's kingdom other than by repentance and the acceptance of the blood of Jesus Christ as sacrifice for our sin; once one has done that, they have entered the kingdom of God. While here on earth, we obviously don't have the kingdom of God as we will when we enter heaven and experience the kingdom in its fullness. Simply stated, the kingdom of God is the rule of God in our lives now.

The purpose of God in bringing Israel out of bondage and into the promised land, a land "flowing with milk and honey" was to show his power and provision to all the nations of the world in order to draw those nations to himself. This is the same purpose God has for his bride, his followers, the church; to be examples and guides to others in order to bring all people into his kingdom.

Whether it was the Israelites of the Old Testament or the church of the New Testament, there are requirements to be blessed and prospered by God. Deuteronomy, chapters 28 through 30, lays it all out, beginning in Deuteronomy 28:1: *If you fully obey the Lord your God and carefully follow all His commands I give you today, the Lord your God will set you high above all the nations on earth. All these blessings will come upon you and accompany you if you obey the Lord your God.*

There are two big *if*s in those two verses, and God goes on with a big *however* in verse 15 of chapter 28: *However, if you do not obey the Lord your God and do not* *carefully follow all His commands and decrees I am giving you today, all these curses will come upon you and overtake you.* The list of problems they will have is long and covers the rest of chapter 28.

Deuteronomy 30 wraps it all up. Beginning at verse 15, God clearly states that they have a choice to make. Israel can choose between "life and prosperity" or "death and destruction." Beginning in verse 19, God reiterates their choices. He says: *"I have set before you life and death, blessings and curses. Now choose life."*

Whether it is Israel going into the promised land or sinners repenting and going into God's kingdom, there are two major similarities: first, the work is God's; second, Israel and the Church must be obedient to God and his ways in order to fully take possession of the land. God's people have a responsibility; failure to carry out that responsibility will result in trouble and grief. The good news is that God gives his people everything they need to do the job; the bad news is that humans want to do their own thing, even though God's ways are the best and guarantee the best results.

The book of Joshua tells of the conquest of the land of Canaan, the promised land. It also tells of the enemy not being completely driven out. Joshua 11:22 says that some of the enemy was left in Gaza, Gath, and Ashdod. What is the result of the enemy being left in the land? Gaza is where Samson was defeated, Gath produced Goliath, and the ark of the covenant was captured and taken to Ashdod. Wherever and whenever the Israelites failed to completely obey God in driving the enemy out of the land, they paid a price. God told them to get rid of the enemies' gods, customs, and practices. The problem with the Israelites and us today is that we find the ways of the enemy to be attractive. No matter how destructive these ways are, we adopt them and live contrary to God's Word.

One time, Israel allowed the enemy into the land by being deceived. Joshua 9 illustrates the problems that can develop if we don't consult with God on issues in our lives. God knows everything, and we need to consult with him on what is going on; we will pay a price if we don't seek him and his will continually. Just as Israel suffered defeat and trouble for allowing the ways of the enemy to permeate their society, Christians also fail to seek spiritual maturity and Christ-like behavior because of continuing to allow the practices, lifestyles, and philosophies of the anti-God, secular society into our lives.

God brought Israel into the promised land, and he brought believers into his kingdom, but that is just the beginning. Like Israel, we too must drive out the enemy. Who or what is the enemy? The enemy is everything in our lives that fights against the nature of God in us. We cannot participate in the kingdom of God and in the world's system at the same time; the more we have of one, the less we will have of the other. We are to be in the world—we live here, but we are not to be of the world.

I heard a pastor tell about a man who came to him to seek prayer because the man felt compelled to enter the pornographic bookstores and theaters every time he drove down a certain street in his town. The pastor asked him "Do you work on that street?" "No," the man replied. "Do you live on that street?" the pastor asked. Again the man replied, "No." The pastor's reply was simple: "Stay off that street."

We all need to stay off that street. Don't look at pornography, bad movies, bad books, or ungodly TV shows. Stay out of places that could lead you astray, stay away from friends that could take you down; whatever we have and hold of the world's systems will destroy the life of God in us. We are to live in the world, but not to be controlled or infiltrated by the world's ways. The time has come for the church, and we as individuals, to possess the land. Let's get on with the fight—this is war! Until God's kingdom comes in its fullness at the end of this broken, fallen world, we cannot escape the battle that rages between God's kingdom and the kingdom of evil.

The book of Joshua indicates that the Israelites did have times of peace and freedom from enemy activity, just as we do in our war here upon earth. Even in the midst of our battles, God grants us peace and security as we depend completely on him. We must never be afraid of the battles we face, just as Caleb (Joshua 14:6–15) at age 85 believed the Lord would be with him, asked for permission to drive out the powerful Anakites from the hill country—and he did!

Sadly, the book of Judges tells what happened to Israel when another generation grew up and disregarded God and his rules. In the second chapter of Joshua, we find that another generation grew up who did not know God or what he had done for Israel; this generation

refused to give up their evil practices and stubborn ways.
(Judges 2:19) Apparently, their forefathers did not
teach them about God or the history of God working
in their lives and nation.

The same thing is happening in the US. The US
was established and grew on the basis of God's Word.
Yes, there were mistakes and our forefathers were not
perfect, but they did seek God's will and based our
institutions and society upon his Word. Today our
society is coming apart; we are attacked from within
and from without. In my view, we have only one
problem. All the disasters we see are symptoms; the
problem is that we have thrown God and his ways out
of our institutions and society.

As individuals, as families, as a society, and as a
nation; we cannot prosper or even survive if we fail to
follow God and his ways. He has blessed America more
than any country ever, because we followed in his ways.
However, if we do not return to him in repentance, if
we don't "possess the land", we will loose it.

EIGHTEEN

When one looks at the world today, it is difficult to be optimistic. Terror, corruption, greed, famine, natural disasters, broken economies, drug/alcohol abuse, broken families, broken relationships, psychological breakdowns, poverty, disease, wars, a broken US society—all one has to do is turn on TV to see a never-ending list of disasters in addition to the trials and tribulations in our individual lives. Even in America where we have super abundance, a great deal of leisure time, extravagance of food and material possessions, and unlimited entertainment; people are still uptight, nervous, and unfulfilled. Suicide rates and mental disorders are increasing drastically.

In the midst of all the trouble, Americans are generally far better off than the rest of the world. If one has any money saved, a hobby that requires some equipment or supplies, a variety of clothes in one's closet, two cars (in any condition), and live in one's own home, one is in the top 5 percent of the world's wealthy. If one earns more than $50,000 annually, one is in the top 1 percent of the world's income earners. Even US welfare recipients are in the top 20 percent of the world's income earners. Yet there is fear, uncertainty, unrest, and greed. The old expression "Life is tough and then you die" seems more real every day. How do we cope? How do we survive?

I believe things will continue to deteriorate in our county before there will be any improvement, because we rejected God. I believe there will be increased pressures and persecution upon Christians. The key to not only surviving life in victory in this messed up world and also surviving judgment at our death is found in the twelfth chapter of the book of Revelation. There are several ways of interpreting this book, but I believe verse 11 of chapter 12 clearly provides the key to success in living the Christian life. Revelation was written by the Apostle John to Christians who were going through horrific persecution; they were being tortured, killed, estranged from society, and often their own families made life miserable for them because of their commitment to Jesus Christ.

They overcame him by the blood of the lamb and the word of their testimony; they did not love their lives so much as to shrink from death. Revelation 12:11

No matter what we go through on earth today, we have not yet faced (at least in the US) the trouble these early Christians were facing. They made it, not just merely getting by but coming through in victory. In spite of everything being removed from them, they rejoiced in their suffering because they knew this world was not their home; they rejoiced in knowing what was to follow: life with God. In verse 11, the word *overcome* means to come through with glory, heads held high and legal victory. How is this possible? The first point in overcoming is being dependant on the blood of the Lamb (Jesus). Without the sacrifice of Jesus Christ, who paid for our sins in full, and our repentance, there is no victory or new life. There are no religious rules or rituals we can follow to gain the power to live and overcome in victory. Only the sacrificial blood of Jesus and the resulting power and indwelling of the Holy Spirit can get us through the everyday problems and travails and the judgment to come. Without Jesus as Lord of our lives, there is no real peace, joy, sense of fulfillment, nor power to overcome the evil around us.

There are two more points needed to overcome in power, glory, and victory. These two cannot be accomplished without the new birth and infilling of the Holy Spirit. Trying to workout two and three without the experience of the first element is not only useless but impossible.

The second point is that they overcame evil by the word of their testimony. There are three Greek words used in the New Testament that are translated into *word*. The first is *graphe*; it usually refers to writings, we get our word *graphite* from this word. The second is *rhema*; it usually refers to the spoken word. I had assumed that *rhema* was the word used in this passage because from my own experience in teaching flying and golf, I had found that by teaching, I gain more in knowledge and reinforcement of my own skills. I was wrong—the word used here is *logos*. The Greek word *logos* is usually translated into *word* (ie, John 1:1, *In the beginning was the logos (word) and the logos was with God, and the logos was God)*. In this passage in John 1, the *logos* refers to Jesus, but there is much more. *Logos* also means intelligence, knowledge, power, rationality—in short, the whole essence of something. In John 1:1, Jesus is the whole essence of God, equal with God, God himself.

The use of *logos* in Revelation 12:11 really got my attention. Obviously, speaking what we believe does give us strength and encouragement. Jesus said that he will acknowledge before God those who acknowledge him before men. That is a very good thing, to say the least! But there is more than just our speaking of our faith; we must live it before the world. This means we must be different from the world around us. Our lives must show the essence of Jesus, we must be like him.

The word for *testimony* in Greek is *marturia* (martyr), which means to give witness or testify about, to be of good report, to exhort, and to give reproof or correction. As Christians, we are to live God's Word always and in all aspects of our lives.

In our neighborhoods, clubs, and workplaces we can not act like everyone else. If we do the same complaining, worrying, and use the same foul language of those around us and follow their ungodly habits, philosophies, and worldview, our testimony is compromised or destroyed. By living according to God's Word in the midst of a fallen world, we will stand out like beacons of light and draw others out of sin into God's kingdom. Jesus has called us to be the "light of the world". Each of us needs to ask this question: are we drawing people to God by our lives, or are we verifying in their minds that God is of no consequence?

By our lifestyle and attitudes, we should be proving to the world about us that the Christian lifestyle is more fulfilling and peaceful despite conflicts and trouble in the world.

In a sense, we are passing judgment on those who do not believe. Consider the soldier who keeps his shoes shined, uniform clean, carries himself in a military manner, and conforms to the regulations and customs of his unit. Without saying a word or in any way pointing out other soldiers' lack of soldierly discipline, he passes judgment by showing that proper behavior is possible. By living a life of integrity, honesty, peace, joy, contentment, and self-sacrifice in the midst of chaos, we show everyone around us that the world's system is left wanting and that there is a far superior way of life. The more we abide in God and in his Word, the stronger, more effective we will become in being a witness for God.

The apostle Peter tells us: *Always be prepared to give an answer to everyone who asks you to give the reason for the hope you have* (1 Peter 3:15). It is not enough to simply tell others what God has done for us, although this is a great starting point. We must be able to give sound, logical answers as to why we believe as we do. In today's society, where the concept of universal truth has been abandoned, when one tells another about what God has done for them, the response is likely to be, "Well, that's fine for you, but I have my own truth that works for me."

Many people today hang onto their beliefs because they have a vested interest in their worldview and subsequent lifestyles. Their position is valuable to them, and they do not want to change. As soldiers of God, we need to attack their position, drive them from their position, and then defend the position of truth from their counterattacks. We need to become apologists for God's Word and kingdom.

The third point to living an overcoming victorious life in spite of all the mess around us is the last phrase of verse 11: *They did not love their lives so much as to shrink from death.* First, the early Christians and all those who have been persecuted since (more have died for Christ in the past one hundred years than in all the years before), believed life on this earth was brief, temporary, and of little consequence compared to the unspeakable joy of being with God forever in a perfect, wonderful place.

However, looking again at the Greek word for life adds a great deal to understanding this passage more fully. One Greek word for life is *bios*, a word that does not appear in the Greek New Testament. We get our word *biology* from this word. Another Greek word for life is *zoe*, this means eternal life or full life with God. When we accept Jesus sacrifice by repenting of our sins and inviting him to live in us, we enter eternal life at that time. Our bodies will die, but our eternal soul has already entered eternal life.

The word for life used in this passage is *psyche*. From this word, we get psychology and psychiatry. *Psyche* refers to our will, volition, desires, and rationality. Our will being submitted to God results in the most complete life possible. We will become all God wants us to be and produce the most stimulating, fulfilling, productive life possible in the middle of everything. This does not mean life will be easy or full of prosperity and health. It does mean that Almighty God, who created the entire universe from nothing, will be our constant companion, friend, guide, mentor, provider, and sustainer. Believe it or not, he knows more than we do and can do everything better than we can.

The fundamental problem is that we humans want to be our own god and not listen to anything or anyone that presents a message or direction we do not want. We are basically self-centered and self-indulgent. The only way we can ever get to the point of being completely and unreservedly committed to God is to deal with our sinful nature. The "old man" cannot be fixed by religion or man-made programs—it must die! Paul said in Romans 6:6, *For we know that our old self was crucified with Him so that the body of sin might be rendered powerless, that we should no longer be slaves to sin.*

We usually think of sin as wrongdoing; in reality, sin is wrong being. The old man which Paul refers to is our sinful nature which wants to be in control. We must decide as a matter of our free will that our sinful nature has to die. We need to make a decision to live God's life or our own life. The more we have of one the less we'll have of the other.

Oswald Chambers in the April 10 daily reading asks this question, "Have you entered into the glorious privilege of being crucified with Christ, until all that remains in your flesh and blood is his life?" He then goes on to quote Galatians 2:20: *I have been crucified with Christ; it is no longer I who live, but Christ lives in me.*

Paul in Romans 6:11–12 sums it up when he writes: *Count yourselves dead to sin but alive to God in Christ Jesus. Therefore do not let sin reign in your mortal body so that you obey its evil desires.*

The decision to submit and commit to God is not a one time act; it must become a daily, lifelong journey, a lifestyle of allowing his life to be lived and expressed in ours. Somehow we think that death to self and submission to God will make us miserable; in reality, it is our life away from God that leads to all the grief. God cares for us more than anyone. He has all power, knowledge, and wisdom; to ignore him is way beyond stupid—it is insane!

In my seventy years, I have seen a tremendous difference in the lives of those who are committed to God and those who are committed to self and the ways of this fallen world. Those whom I have seen follow God have peace, joy, fulfillment, and contentment in the face of trouble and pain. Those who follow the world are generally a mess; they may look okay on the outside, but there is no peace, joy, fulfillment, or contentment.

There are only two unavoidable choices that can be made, and everyone will decide which way to go: one can accept God's ways, or one can accept the ways of the world. Accept God and enjoy eternal life with the Creator. Accept the world, and one will spend eternity in remorse, torment, without peace, without joy, without comfort, and without companionship. I believe hell is solitary confinement.

There is nothing in this world worth hanging onto. Give him your life and everything in it. The way to victory is the way of God. Our way has been contaminated with the way of the world.

NINETEEN

The study and investigation that began upon the raising of the questions listed in chapter ten has slowed down but does continue. Everything I see, read, analyze, and study reinforces the conclusions I have written in this book.

God, a Trinity, created the universe and everything in it. Man, created in the image of God, rebelled and entered a state of separation from God. Jesus, eternal God, took upon his divine nature human flesh, and by his death, paid for man's rebellion against God. By the resurrection from the dead, Jesus made it possible for believers to be reunited into an everlasting life in relationship with God.

In the midst of trouble, sickness, disaster, and persecution; God is always there. He works out everything for the best in the lives of those who commit to him and obey him; this will result in a sense of deep inner peace and joy. We will not always see or understand all that is taking place in our lives, but we can take comfort in knowing that he knows and that we are under his care, guidance, and protection. God is developing and teaching us; he is maturing us in faith and conforming us to his nature.

All Christians need to make a deeper commitment and get fully involved in God's work in spite of the difficulties. Being 100 percent committed has its own rewards and sense of fulfillment. Prior to my being wounded in Vietnam, I had been to Marine Corps birthday balls and I enjoyed it—the ceremony, celebration, sense of history, and fellowship were great. However, after having been "blooded" in war, the next birthday ball I went to took on a much deeper and larger meaning. Is the danger and cost of being fully involved worth it? Yes, indeed! I'd do it all over again in a minute. Get into the fight, Christian!

Of course, the fight is rough! Politics is dirty, government is corrupt, schools are teaching garbage—that's why God wants you there in the fight. As a youngster, I remember being told by teachers that politics was dirty and the military was a rough bunch; therefore, as Christians, we needed to avoid those and other professions. Wrong! Things got dirty because Christians failed to get involved. The church must have more influence in our society and in our institutions. Our Founding Fathers agreed that the only way a republic could survive is if its people and government followed God's Word.

Every job is important in God's eyes; the one who pumps gas into an airplane is no less a person than the one who pilots it or orders parts for it or installs the parts—each team member is important. In our churches, we put pastors and elders on pedestals—this is wrong. Yes, they are to be respected and listened to, but all the people need to be involved because every position, job, or other contributions to the effectiveness of the church are vital to its health. Every member needs to be looking for a way into the battle, not for a way out. We need Christians to become involved in all aspects of society; to get off the sidelines, out of the bleachers, and into the fight now! We need people to become judges, politicians, professors, journalists, military—every aspect of our nation needs to get back to a God and Bible-based worldview.

In the fight for a Pacific Ocean island named Tarawa, there is a story of an unnamed marine. In the battle plan, a battalion commander was instructed to have a small flag planted on the assault beach to mark the left flank of his battalion. This order was passed on to the company commander on the left side of the battalion, who then passed it on to the platoon commander on the left side of the company. The platoon commander passed the order on to the squad leader on the left side of the platoon, who passed the order to a marine on the left side of the squad.

No one knows what the squad leader said, but it probably went something like this: "Marine, when you get off the —— landing craft, you place this —— flag on the —— beach. The marines in the second wave need to know where we are. Don't shoot your —— rifle or throw a —— grenade until you plant the —— flag! Got it?" After the battle, the private was found facedown on the beach. He was riddled with bullets; his hand was still on the flag planted where it was supposed to be planted. A comment made by a general while touring the battle site and upon observing the body of the dead marine said that men like that would never be defeated.

There was another reason the marines were able to take Tarawa. Many of the leaders were incapacitated or killed early in the fighting, leaving large numbers of marines leaderless; but this did not stop or slow down the battle. When squads and platoons ceased to exist, small groups of marines continued to fight, often going into the enemies bunkers to take them on hand to hand. They were committed to doing their job no matter the cost. Yes, we need senior officers for the overall planning and execution of the war, but it takes a lot of soldiers/citizens to get the job done.

I believe there may come a time in the US when many churches will become a thing of the past and many leaders will be "out of business." When that time comes, it will be incumbent upon individual Christians to come together to press on with our duty to be lights to the world; however, this cannot happen unless we are fellowshipping now. It is too late to equip and organize once the battle has begun.

Only God knows if more marines would have lost their lives if the unknown marine had failed to plant the flag. Only God knows how important the life of every Christian is, and the impact of each Christian's life. Regardless of one's ability, learning, age, experience; everyone needs to become involved, everyone is important, everyone has a place in God's kingdom. We are in a war and everyone on the team who isn't committed to the supreme commander and to the mission, or is in any way involved with "civilian" entanglements, will drag us all down. We are here to occupy until he comes or we go, whether that is tomorrow or five hundred years from now. Don't look for a way out. Don't count the days. Do your job until your hitch is over. Things are not always going to be prosperous and wonderful. Just suck it up and stay in the fight—He'll never leave you!

Over the years, I began to recognize how much the military life and the Christian life are similar. The military life is about training and preparation for conducting and winning wars. To fight and win, one must be conditioned; one needs physical and emotional strength; one needs knowledge of weapons, tactics, and to be familiar with the enemies' weapons and ways. This does not come without effort;—there needs to be study, tough training, exertion, and being "pounded into the dirt" once in awhile.

Unfortunately, unlike the marines with whom I lived, trained, and fought, the church in the US is poorly trained, educated, equipped, organized, and lacking in commitment to the task set out before us by Jesus. The church is a mess and is not in a position to have the needed impact on society because we are not living according to the Word of God. We are not combat-ready.

A large number of Christians are following the teachers who appear on TV, proclaiming that as believers we should experience only blessing upon blessing of prosperity—a well-being and trouble free life. This is contrary to the teaching of Jesus. Yes, there are blessings of peace and joy in the midst of trouble, but as stated earlier, if one follows Jesus, there will be persecution because of the hate shown to anything or anyone representing God.

Many Christians also believe that the church will be taken to heaven before the world really becomes a mess, so they are not concerned with the possibility of serious persecution. This belief has a devastating impact on a believers' readiness to be totally engaged in the current "war." I would hate to go into combat with someone who is untrained, unfit (mentally and physically), and who really wants to avoid the fight.

One of the saddest chapters in American military history involves many of the American soldiers captured by the communists during the Korean War. Never in any other American war has such a large number of Americans turned against their country and fellow soldiers. The reasons were that they were inadequately prepared, physically, mentally, and in general military training. They did not fully comprehend the cause for which they were fighting, they did not understand the nature of the United States or of the communists. As a result, they lacked commitment and were easily turned to the communists' side. I see the same scenario in the church in the United States.

Today, Christians are the most persecuted people on earth, they are being imprisoned, tortured, and killed; they are thrown out of their homes and villages. In the US, we have not yet reached those extreme persecutions, but Christians are singled out; there are many reports of Christian students in state schools, colleges, and universities who are being regularly ridiculed, intimidated, harassed, and demeaned for their beliefs.

In the media and entertainment industries, Christians are fair game. The only moral standard that is allowed to be mentioned in these areas is tolerance. Apparently, tolerance applies to all belief systems and lifestyles except any expression of faith in God, his Word, or any expression of an idea that says it is possible that there is supernatural design or any intelligence behind creation.

The secular worldview, which is the only one permitted in any public forum is diametrically opposed to the worldview held by Christians. There can be no compromise; there will be no peace unless the Christians shut up and go away. The God-denying worldview is violently opposed to God's ways, his standards, and his people. The secular worldview is in control of the government, courts, media, entertainment industry, and education system.

We also face a shooting war against radical Islam, which is committed to destroying everything outside of itself. I also believe we'll see riots and civil unrest from groups within our country. Our society is breaking up with a multitude of minority interest groups demanding special consideration from the government—this is a disaster in waiting. The Christian worldview, which has provided more liberty and freedom for more people than any system ever, is under attack from within and without.

The Christian life is about warfare. In John 15:18, Jesus stated: *If the world hates you, keep in mind that it hated me first. If you belonged to the world, it would love you as its own. As it is, you do not belong to the world, but I have chosen you out of the world. That is why the world hates you. Remember the words I spoke to you: 'No servant is greater than his master.' If they persecuted me, they will persecute you also.*

God has an army—the church which is composed of all believers. God also has a mission—to reach the lost with his word. As in the military, there are a multitude of tasks and positions necessary to accomplish the mission. In order for individual Christians to be useful and to accomplish the purpose in God's army for which God has designed and equipped them, I believe there are two fundamental requirements.

First, all believers need to have a healthy fear and awe of God. June Gunden in "The Woman's Study Bible", when referring to I Chronicles 16:8-36, says that to really understand what the fear of God is all about, we need to take time away from ourselves and concentrate on God. We must also face up to the fact that the world doesn't revolve about us, our lives must be in God's hands. She added that we must understand God's holiness, power and deep love, and our lack of holiness, power and love.

When I look at God's fantastic creation, the massive, finely tuned universe, the human body, and the incredibly diverse life forms, I am awe struck. When I consider that the eternal, all powerful, all knowing holy God came here to this earth to pay for my sin by a horrific death, I am overwhelmed.

There is only one response on our part that makes any sense, and that is the second requirement to be used by God. When we consider who God is and who we are, the only appropriate response is to totally commit all we are and all we have to him. During our brief life on earth, there is nothing we can acquire or accomplish that can come close to the riches to be found in God's kingdom.

Unfortunately, many Christians feel that they don't have the training or education to be used in God's kingdom. They believe they do not have value, talent or capability necessary to be used in what God is doing. In reality, the believer who has the fear and awe of God, and the commitment to serve him will be equipped and directed by God—and that is far superior to what any Bible class, school or seminary can provide.

Over the years, since I was a teenager, the question was: what job does God want me to do, and where does he want me to do it? I have come to realize that this is not the major question concerning the will of God in our lives. The best answer to the question of God's will comes from a daily devotional book written by Oswald Chambers (1874–1917) and edited to modern English by James Reimann. The book is *"My Utmost For His Highest"*, a book I've been reading daily for over thirty years, I highly recommend it.

In the January 14 reading, Oswald says that the call of God is not just for a small select group to a few positions. The call of God goes out to all believers. Unfortunately, many are not listening because they feel that they are unworthy or unqualified to do anything in God's kingdom.

In the January 16th meditation, there are two major points I would like to point out; first, we need to know the nature of God and commit to him in order for his nature to be in us. If God's nature is not in us, there will be no communication. The second point is that if we dwell on our own qualities, traits, and abilities, we'll never hear from God. A good example of this is in my own life. As a pilot, I assumed God would send me someplace to fly planes in some sort of missionary work, but he had totally different plans. The fact is that if we try to do God's work in our own strength, we will not depend on him—and that leads to defeat. Only by dying to self and accepting his life in us will we be able to hear him and follow him. Too many Christians, especially leaders, trust too much in their training, preparations and their own abilities, therefore they fail to listen to and follow God.

The January 17th meditation is a continuation of the previous day's reading in that in order to receive direction and guidance from God, we need to have the heart of a servant. If we love him and are devoted to him, our service "becomes a natural part of my life," to quote Mr. Chambers.

This oneness with God only comes through commitment of our life and time to him. This will not happen in one hour a week in church and a two-minute prayer as we collapse into bed each night; this must become a lifestyle. In all we do—being with family and friends, gardening, working, golfing, a walk through the woods or down a street—we will be at peace and be full of joy if we are continuing to enjoy his presence and his creation. Thanking him and praising him for everything in all circumstances leads to a deep sense of inner peace and joy that the world doesn't understand and can not take away. If we are totally devoted to him, he will direct, guide, counsel, correct, and be our constant companion, and we will be fulfilled in a way the world can not touch.

Dear reader, I don't care if you are fifteen, fifty or eight-five. I don't care about what you have done or not done. Please, do not look at yourself as being unlovable, useless, incapable, untalented, uneducated or in any way inadequate to be accepted and used by God. I only care that you will repent of your sin and receive a new life from Jesus and a permanent relationship with the Almighty God, the Creator of the universe.

When you give up your old self, God will take you into a new life that you didn't think would be possible. There will be difficulty and trouble, but in the midst of life on this troubled planet, you will experience an inner peace, joy and contentment you never had before. In your new life he'll guide and equip you for the duty he designed for you, and he'll take care of the results.

BIBLIOGRAPHY

Behe, Michael J.—*Darwin's Black Box,* New York, NY, The Free Press, 1996

Chambers, Oswald—Edited by James Reimann, *My Utmost for His Highest,* Grand Rapids, MI, Discovery House, 1992

Copan, Paul and William Lane Craig—*Creation Out of Nothing,* Grand Rapids, MI, Baker, 2004

Craig, William Lane—*On Guard,* Colorado Springs, CO, David C. Cook, 2010

Dembski, William A. and Michael R. Licoma—*Evidence for God,* Grand Rapids, MI, Baker, 2010

Dembski, William A.—*Intelligent Design,* Downers Grove, IL, InterVarsity Press, 1999

Federer, William J.—*America's God and Country,* Wheaton, IL, Tyndale House, 1996

Geisler, Norman L.—*Baker Encyclopedia of Christian Apologetics,* Grand Rapids, MI, Baker, 1999

Geisler, Norman L. and Ronald M. Brooks—*Come, Let Us Reason,* Grand Rapids, MI, Baker, 1990

Geisler, Norman L. and Frank Turek—*I Don't Have Enough Faith To Be An Atheist*, Wheaton, IL, Crossway Books, 2004

Geisler, Norman L. and Patrick Zukeran—*The Apologetics of Jesus*, Grand Rapids, MI, Baker, 2009

Geisler, Norman L. and Peter Bocchino—*Unshakable Foundations*, Minneapolis, MN, 2001

Geisler, Norman L. and Ron Brooks—*When Skeptics Ask*, Grand Rapids, MI, Baker, 1990

Hanegraaff, Hank—*The Bible Answer Book*, Nashville, TN, Thomas Nelson, 2004

Hart, Benjamin—*Faith and Freedom*, Ottawa, IL, Jameson Books, 1988

Huse, Scott M.—*The Collapse of Evolution*, Grand Rapids, MI, Baker, 1983

Johnson, Phillip E.—*Darwin On Trial*, Downers Grove, IL, InterVarsity Press, 1991

Johnson, Phillip E.—*The Right Questions*, Downers Grove, IL, InterVarsity Press, 2002

Johnson, Phillip E.—*The Wedge of Truth*, Downers Grove, IL, InterVarsity Press, 2000

Kreeft, Peter and Ronald K. Tacelli—*Handbook of Christian Apologetics*, Downers Grove, IL, InterVarsity Press, 1994

Little, Paul E.—*Know Why You Believe*, Downers Grove, IL, InterVarsity Press, 2000

Marshall, Peter and David Manuel—*The Glory of America*, Bloomington, MN, Garborg's Heart 'N Home, 1991

Marshall, Peter and David Manuel—*The Light and The Glory*, Old Tappan, NJ, F.H. Revell, 1977

McDowell, Josh—*Beyond Belief To Convictions*, Carol Stream, IL, Tyndale House, 2002

McDowell, Josh—*The New Evidence That Demands A Verdict*, Nashville, TN, Thomas Nelson, 1999

McFarland, Alex—*The 10 Most Common Objections To Christianity*, Ventura, CA, Regal Books, 2007

McGrath, Alister E.—*Intellectuals Don't Need God*, Grand Rapids, MI, Zondervan, 1993

Myers, John (compiled by)—*Voices From the Edge of Eternity*, New Kensington, PA, Whitaker House, 1998

Rana, Fazale and Hugh Ross—*Origins Of Life*, Colorado Springs, CO, NAVPRESS, 2004

Ross, Hugh Ph.D.—*Beyond the Cosmos*, Colorado Springs, CO, NAVPRESS, 1996

Ross, Hugh Ph.D.—*Creation As Science*, Colorado Springs, CO, NAVPRESS, 2006

Ross, Hugh Ph.D.—*The Creator and the Cosmos*, Colorado Springs, CO, NAVPRESS, 1993

Samples, Kenneth Richard—*A World of Difference*, Grand Rapids, MI, Baker, 2007

Samples, Kenneth Richard—*Without A Doubt*, Grand Rapids, MI, Baker, 2004

Sarfati, Jonathan, Ph.D—*Refuting Evolution*, Australia, 2002

Schaeffer, Francis A.—*The Complete Works of Francis A. Schaeffer*, Wheaton, IL, Crossway Books, 1982

Schwarzkopf, Norman L. General—*It Doesn't Take A Hero*, New York, NY, Bantam Books, 1992

Seeds, Michael A.—*Foundations of Astronomy*, USA, Wadsworth Publishing, 1997

Simmons, Geoffrey MD—*What Darwin Didn't Know*, Eugene, OR, Harvest House, 2004

Sproul, R.C.—*Not A Chance*, Grand Rapids, MI, Baker, 1994

Sproul, R.C.—*Tearing Down Strongholds*, Phillipsburg, NJ, P & R Publishing, 2002

Strobel, Lee—*The Case for Christ*, Grand Rapids, MI, Zondervan, 1998

Strobel, Lee—*The Case for a Creator*, Grand Rapids, MI, Zondervan, 2004

Strobel, Lee—*The Case for Easter*, Grand Rapids, MI, Zondervan, 1998

Strobel, Lee—*The Case for Faith*, Grand Rapids, MI, Zondervan, 2000

The Woman's Devotional Bible, Grand Rapids, MI, Zondervan, 1990